ESSENTIAL ELEMENTS for Strings

COMPREHENSIVE STRING METHOD

MICHAEL ALLEN • ROBERT GILLESPIE • PAMELA TELLEJOHN HAYES
ARRANGEMENTS BY JOHN HIGGINS

CONGRATULATIONS! You have made one of the most rewarding decisions in your life by joining the orchestra. The key to succeeding with *Essential Elements for Strings* is your commitment to daily practice. Each time you learn a new note, count a new rhythm, or play a melody with a friend, you become a more accomplished musician. As you continue to develop your skills, you will become increasingly aware of an abundance of opportunities that are available in the future. Musicians can teach, perform, conduct, or compose. No matter what profession you choose there are always opportunities available to you. You can play in community, civic, or church orchestras, attend concerts, and become a supporter of the arts. Whether you choose music as a vocation or avocation, we hope it will become an important part of your life. We are thrilled to welcome you to our orchestra family and wish you the very best for a lifetime of musical success.

HISTORY OF THE CELLO

The string family includes the violin, viola, violoncello, and the double bass. The early ancestors of the violin were the Arabian rebab and rebec, popular during the 14th–16th centuries. During the 1500s, there were two types of viols: the viola da gamba, played on the knee, and the viola da braccia, played on the shoulder.

The sound of the violoncello, called 'cello' for short, is pitched an octave below the viola. The cello has a warm tone and is capable of playing a wide range of dynamics. It is often referred to as the tenor of the orchestra. Antonio Stradivari, and the Guarneri and Guadagnini families were famous instrument makers from the 17th and 18th centuries, and their cellos are still in use today.

Nearly every composer has written music for the cello, including Johann Sebastian Bach, Ludwig van Beethoven, and Peter Ilyich Tchaikovsky. Famous cello performers include Janos Starker, Leonard Rose, Pablo Casals, Yo-Yo Ma, Sheku Kanneh-Mason, Zuill Bailey, Mischa Maisky, Sol Gabetta, and Kermit Moore.

To create an account, visit:
www.essentialelementsinteractive.com

Student Activation Code
E1CE-1096-4878-4761

ISBN 979-835012076-9

THE CELLO

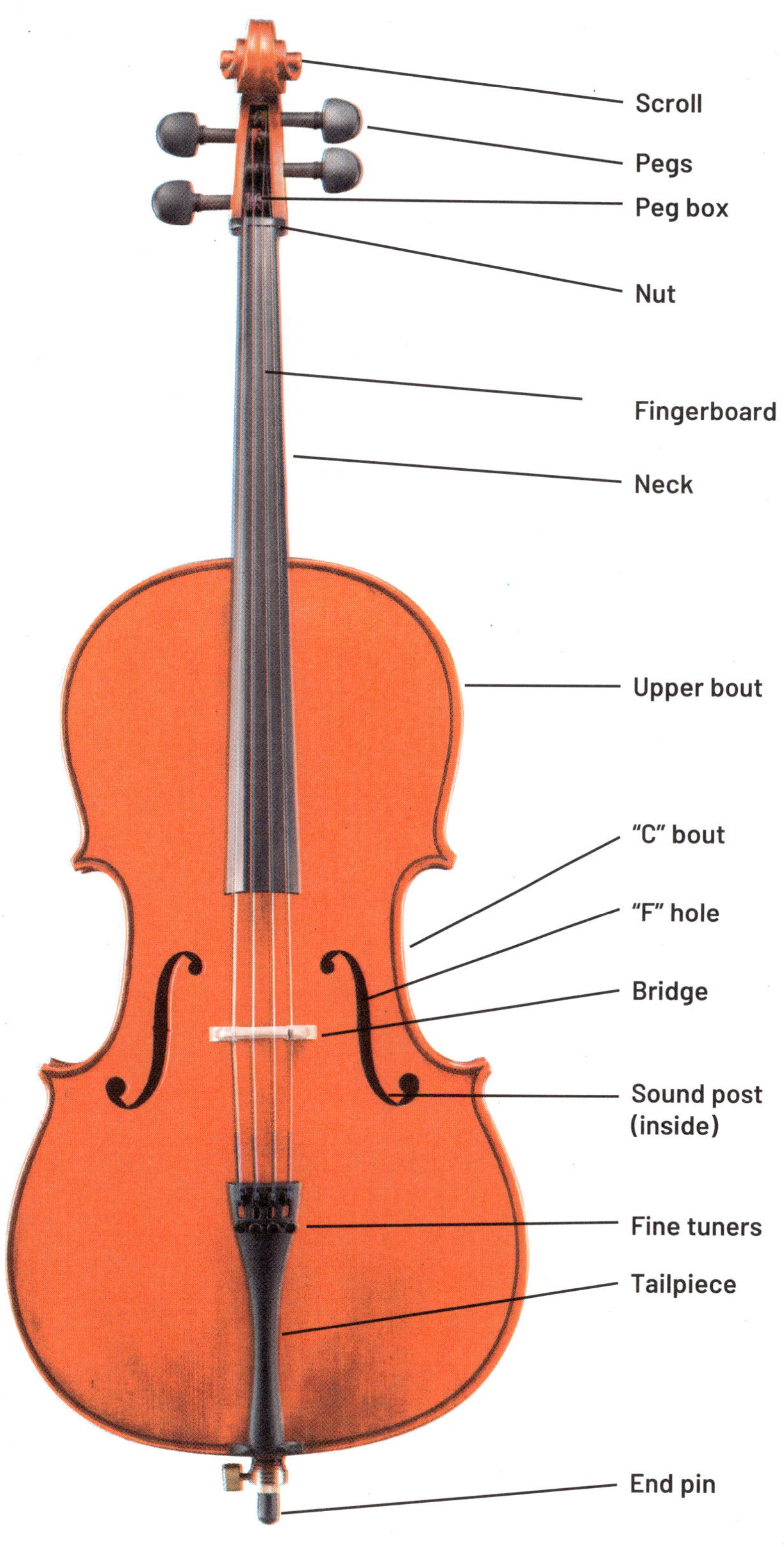

Take Special Care

String instruments are delicate. Follow your teacher's guidelines in caring for your instrument, and it will last forever.

- Follow your teacher's instructions when removing the instrument from the case.
- Protect your instrument from heat, cold, and quick changes in temperature.
- Always wipe off the instrument with a soft dry cloth. Be sure to remove all fingerprints and rosin.

Accessories

- Rosin
- Soft cloth
- Rock stop

Instruments and photos courtesy of Eastman Music Company.

THE BOW

- Never touch the bow hair.

Holding Your Instrument

The best way to learn to play your instrument is to practice one skill at a time. Repeat each step until you are comfortable demonstrating it for your teacher and classmates.

Step 1 Remove the bow from the case and put it in a safe place. Open the case and remove the cello. Identify all parts of the cello.

Step 2 Adjust the length of the end pin so that the scroll of the cello is near your nose when standing.

Step 3 Sit on the front half of your chair with your feet positioned underneath your knees. Place the end pin directly in front of you one arm's length away.

Step 4 Lean the cello slightly to the left and allow the instrument to rest against your chest. The 'C' peg should be near your head behind your left ear, and both knees should touch the cello just below the 'C' bout. It may be necessary to readjust the length or position of the end pin. Identify the letter names of each string: C (lowest pitch), G, D, A. Raise your right index finger over the strings and pluck them as directed by your teacher. Plucking the strings is called *pizzicato*, and is abbreviated *pizz.*

Step 2

Step 3

Step 4

The student shown is a member of the Milwaukee Youth Symphony Orchestra.

THEORY

Beat = The *Pulse* of Music — The **beat** in music should be very steady, just like your pulse.

Quarter Note ♩ = 1 Beat of Sound — **Notes** tell us how high or low to play, and how long to play.

Quarter Rest 𝄽 = 1 Beat of Silence — **Rests** tell us to count silent beats.

Music Staff — The **music staff** has 5 lines and 4 spaces.

Bar Lines — **Bar lines** divide the music staff into **measures**.

Measures — The **measures** on this page have four beats each.

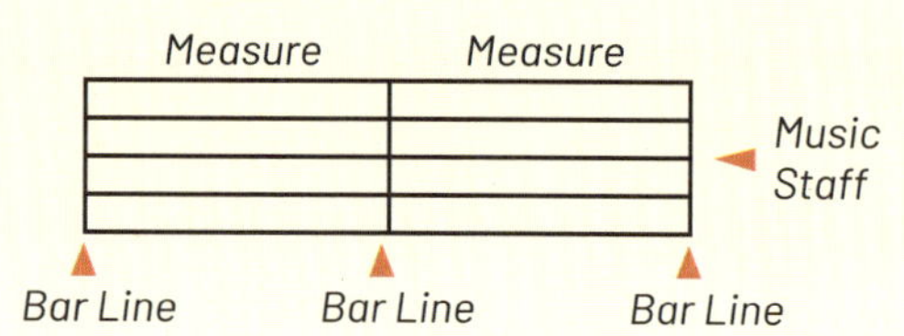

1. TUNING TRACK *Wait quietly for your teacher to tune your instrument.*

2. LET'S PLAY "OPEN D"

Pizzicato (pizz.) ◄ *Pluck the strings*

0 ◄ *Open string*

D

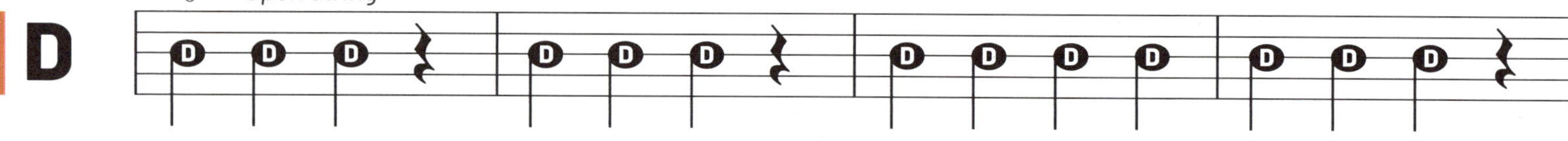

3. LET'S PLAY "OPEN A"

pizz.

0

A

Keep a steady beat.

4. TWO'S A TEAM

pizz.

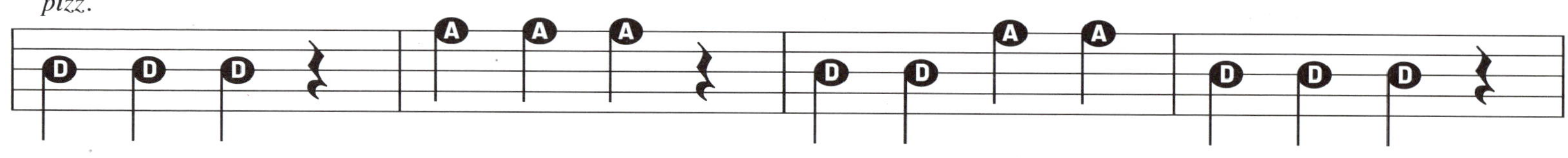

5. AT PIERROT'S DOOR *The melody is included on the online audio.*

pizz.

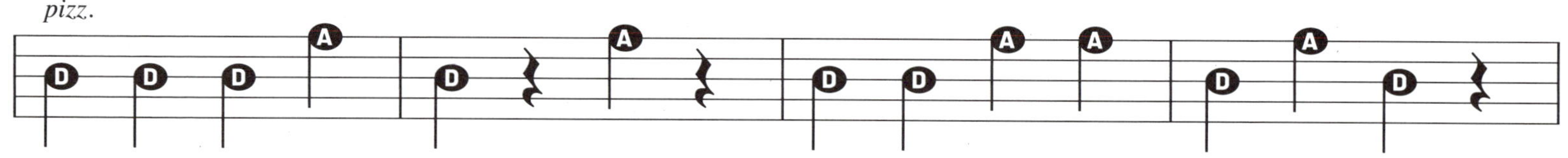

THEORY

Bass Clef

Clefs indicate a set of note names.

Time Signature ***(Meter)***

4/4 — 4 beats per measure; ♩ or 𝄽 gets one beat

The **time signature** tells us how many beats are in each measure and what kind of note gets one beat.

Double Bar

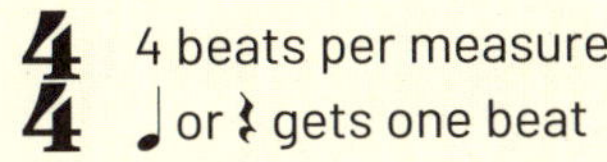

A **double bar** indicates the end of a piece of music.

6. JUMPING JACKS *Identify the clef and time signature before playing.*

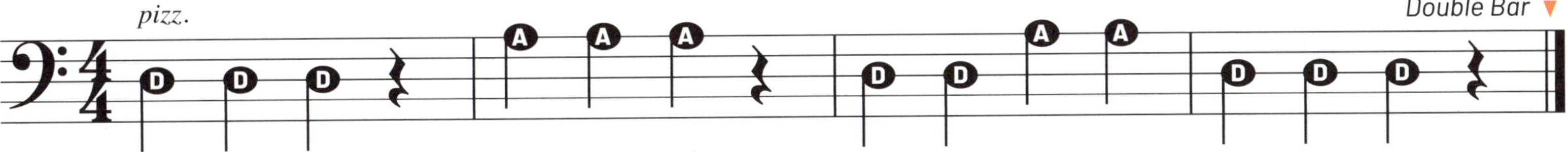

7. MIX 'EM UP

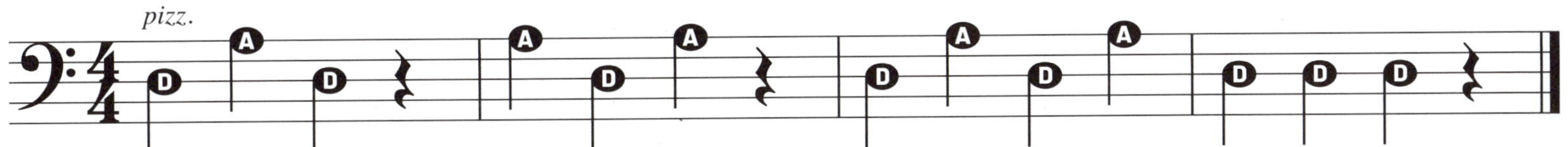

THEORY

Repeat Sign

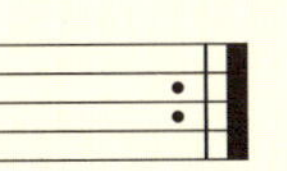

Go back to the beginning and play the music again.

Counting

Count	1	&	2	&	3	&	4	&
Tap	↓	↑	↓	↑	↓	↑	↓	↑

One beat = Tap toe down on the number and up on the "&." Always count when playing or resting.

8. COUNT CAREFULLY *Keep a steady beat when playing or resting.*

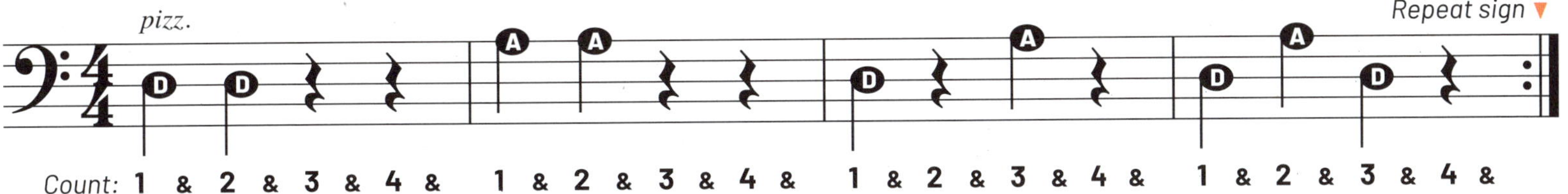

9. ESSENTIAL ELEMENTS QUIZ *Write in the counting before you play.*

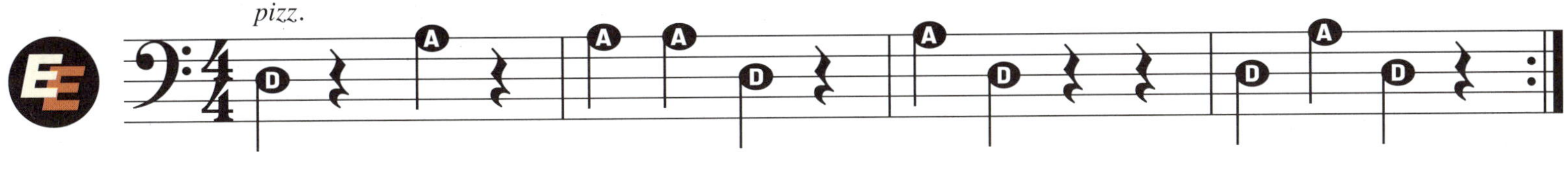

SHAPING THE LEFT HAND

D STRING NOTES

Step 1 Shape your left hand as shown.
Be certain your palm faces you.

0 = Open string
1 = 1st finger
2 = 2nd finger
3 = 3rd finger
4 = 4th finger

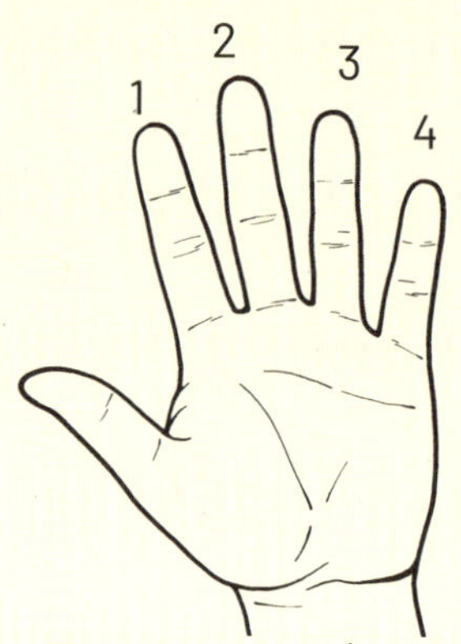

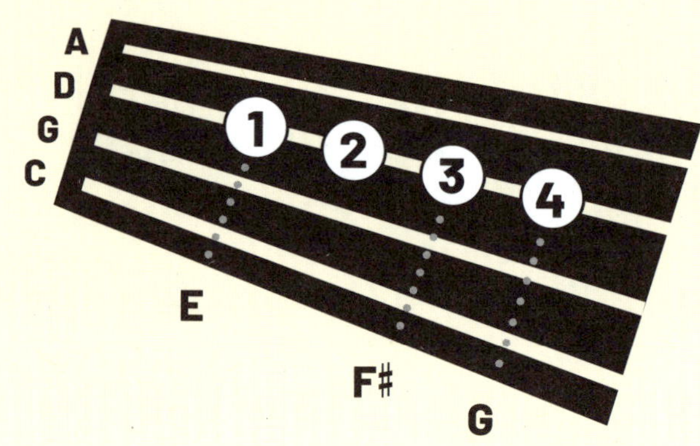

Step 2 Bring your hand to the fingerboard. Place your fingers on the D string, keeping your hand shaped as shown below. Be sure your thumb is behind the 2nd finger and slightly bent.

G is played with 4 fingers on the D string.

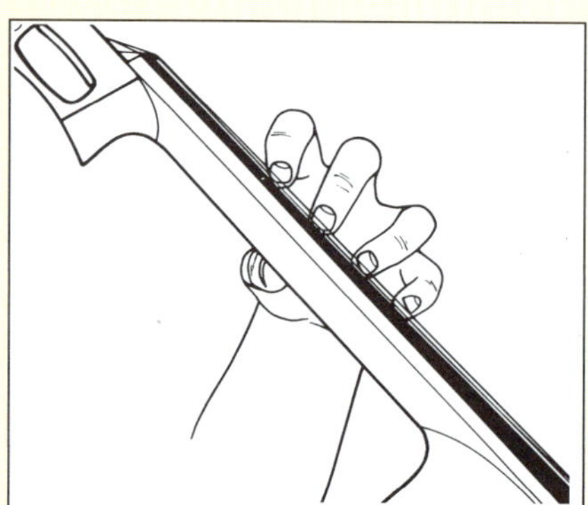

F♯ is played with 3 fingers on the D string.

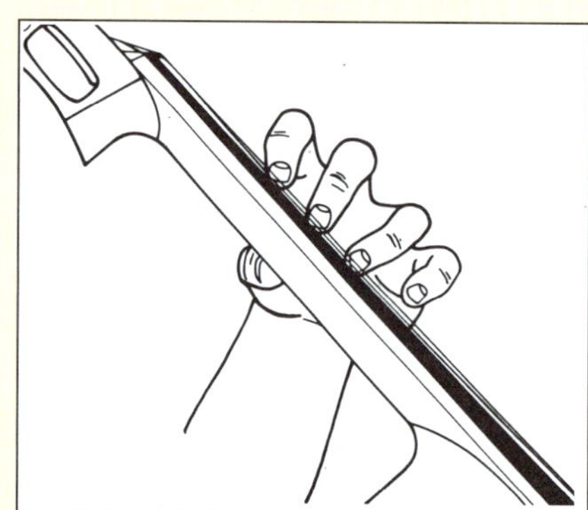

E is played with 1 finger on the D string.

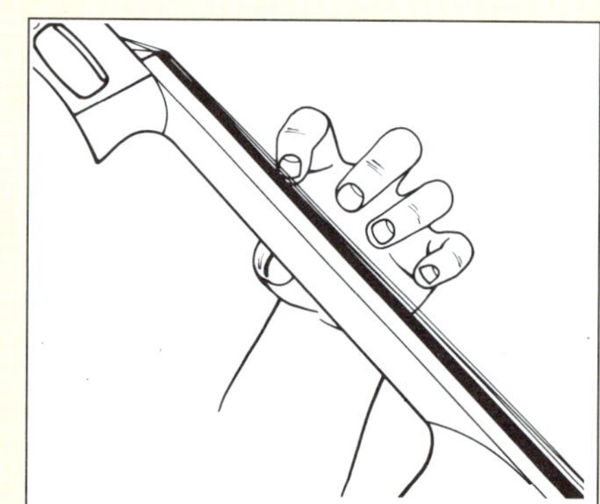

Listening Skills Play what your teacher plays. Listen carefully.

10. LET'S READ "G" *Start memorizing the note names.*

G

THEORY

Sharp ♯ A **sharp** sign raises the sound of notes and remains in effect for the entire measure. Notes without sharps are called **natural** notes.

11. LET'S READ "F♯" (F-sharp)

F♯

Play all F♯'s. Sharps apply to the entire measure.

12. LIFT OFF

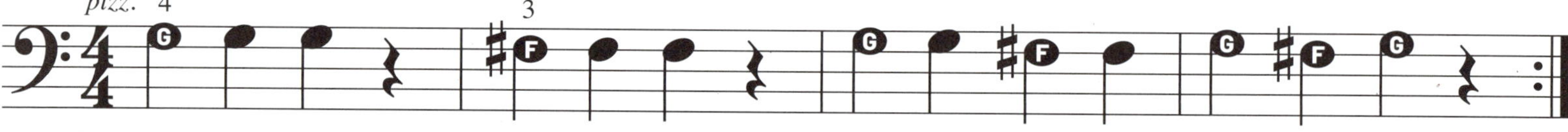

✔ Is your left hand shaped as shown in the diagrams above?

See inside front cover for information on accessing instructional videos.

SHAPING THE RIGHT HAND

BOW BUILDER ONE

Pencil Hold

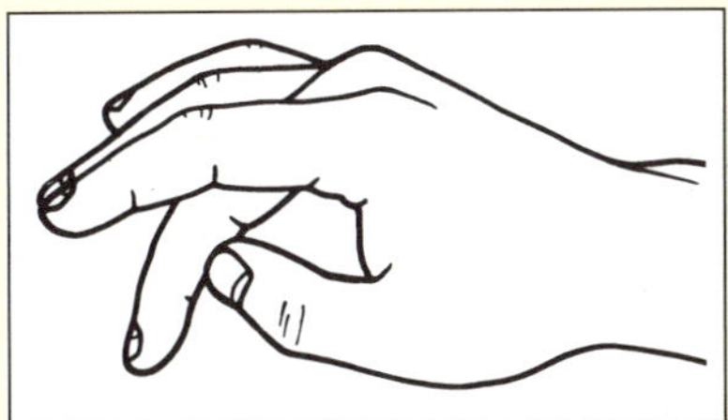

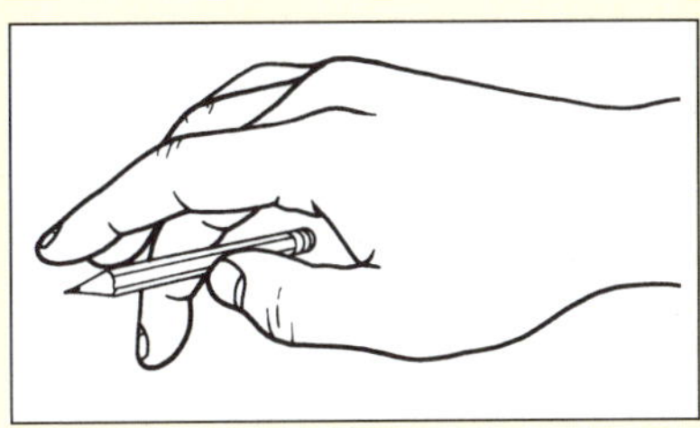

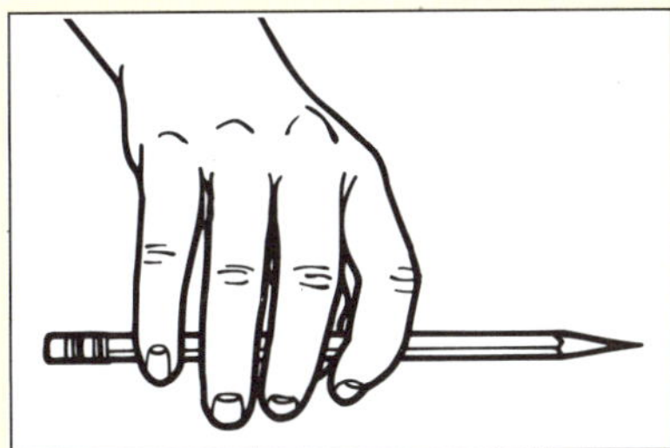

Step 1 Hold a pencil in your left hand about waist level.

Step 2 Place the tip of your right thumb between the first and second joints of your second finger.

Step 3 Place the pencil between your thumb and second finger, while keeping your thumb gently curved.

Step 4 The pencil should touch your first three fingers between the first and second joints, and touch the fourth finger at the first joint, as shown.

Step 5 Remove your left hand from the pencil. Keep your fingers relaxed. Practice shaping your hand on the pencil until it feels natural to you.

Practice BOW BUILDER ONE daily.

13. ON THE TRAIL *Say or sing the note names before you play.*

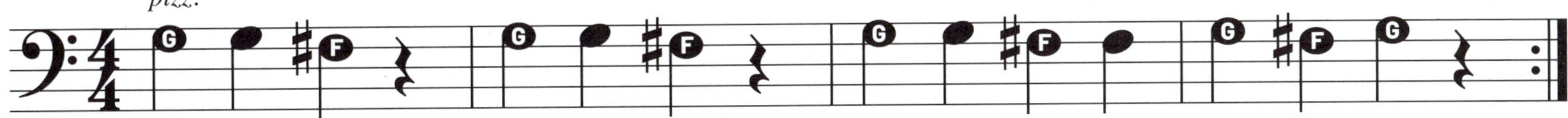

14. LET'S READ "E"

E

15. WALKING SONG

16. ESSENTIAL ELEMENTS QUIZ *Draw the missing symbols where they belong before you play:*

pizz.

G F E D D E F G

BOW BUILDER TWO

Pencil Hold Exercises

I'm Outta Here
Wave good-bye while keeping your wrist relaxed.

Thumb Flexers
Flex your thumb in and out.

Finger Taps
Tap your first finger. Then tap your fourth finger.

Knuckle Turnovers
Turn your hand over and be sure your thumb knuckle is bent, as shown.

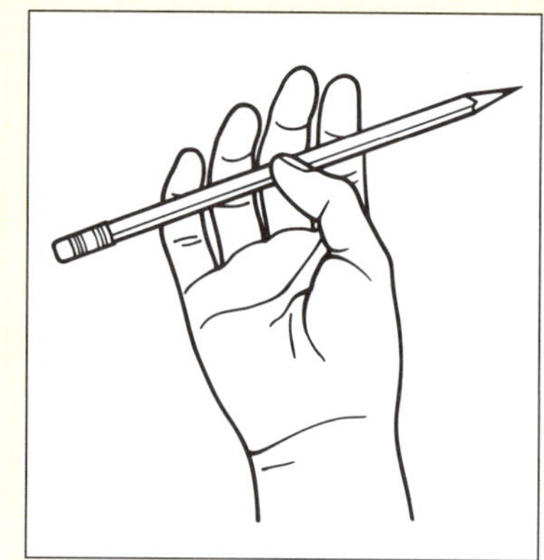

Knuckle Turnovers

BOW BUILDER THREE

Bowing Motions

Elbow Energy

- Swing your right elbow away from your body.
- Open your right forearm, as shown.
- Close your right forearm.
- Swing your elbow back toward your body.

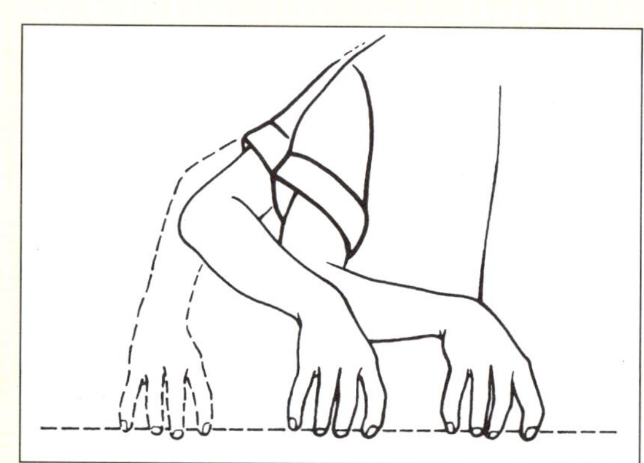

Elbow Energy

17. HOP SCOTCH

HISTORY

Folk songs have been an important part of cultures for centuries and have been passed on from generation to generation. Folk song melodies help define the sound of a culture or region. This folk song comes from the Slavic region of eastern Europe.

18. MORNING DANCE

Slavic Folk Song

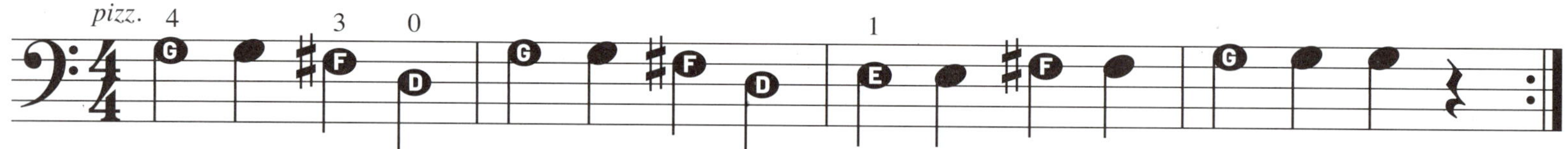

19. ROLLING ALONG

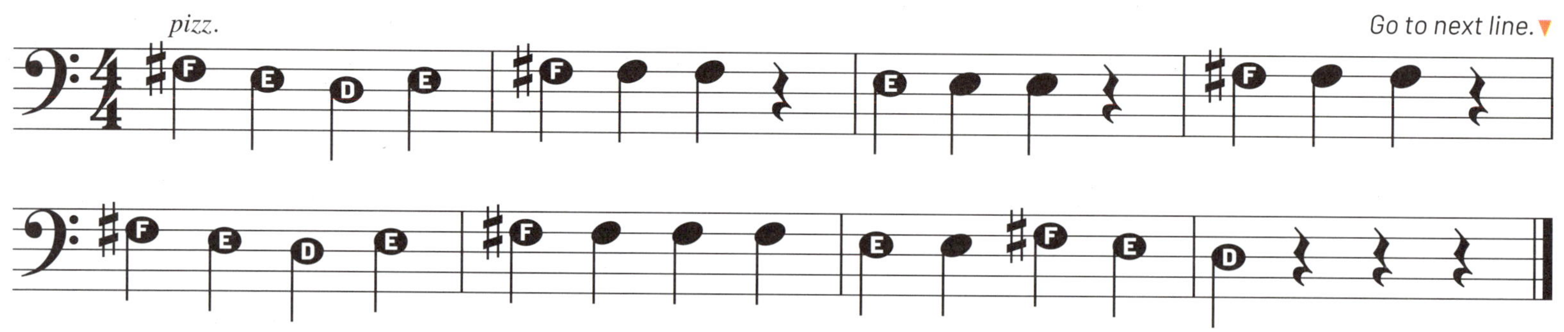

WORKOUTS

Practice the following exercises with your left hand:

Finger Taps 

Tap fingertips on any string. Practice in different combinations of fingers.

Strummin' Along 

Strum the strings with your 4th finger while swinging your elbow, as shown.

20. GOOD KING WENCESLAS

Welsh Folk Song

▲ *Keep fingers down when you see this bracket.*

21. SEMINOLE CHANT

Count: 1 & 2 & 3 & 4 & 1 & 2 & 3 & 4 & 1 & 2 & 3 & 4 & 1 & 2 & 3 & 4 &

22. ESSENTIAL ELEMENTS QUIZ – LIGHTLY ROW

▲ *Prepare F♯ before playing.*

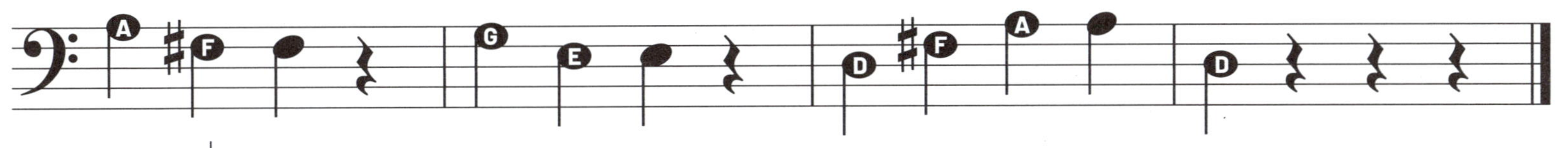

A STRING NOTES

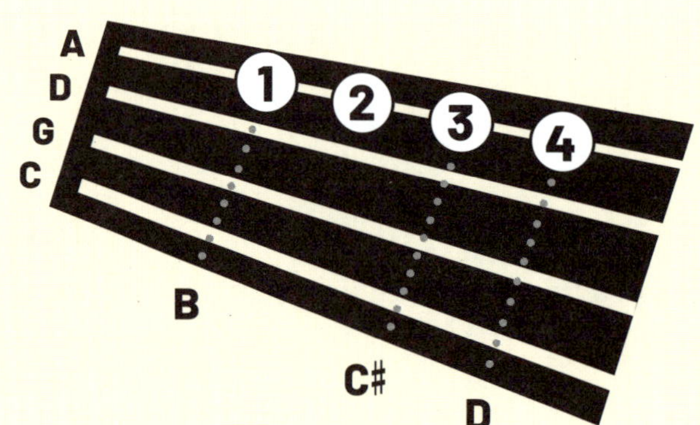

D is played with 4 fingers on the A string.

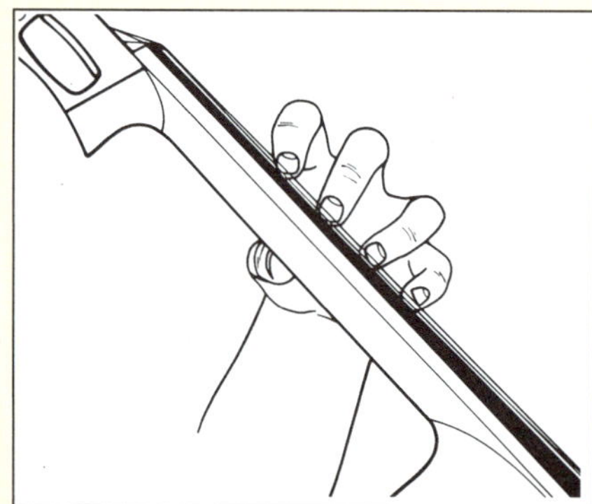

C♯ is played with 3 fingers on the A string.

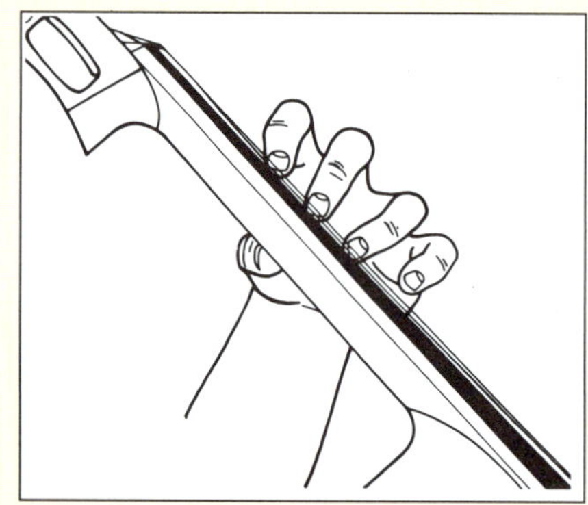

B is played with 1 finger on the A string.

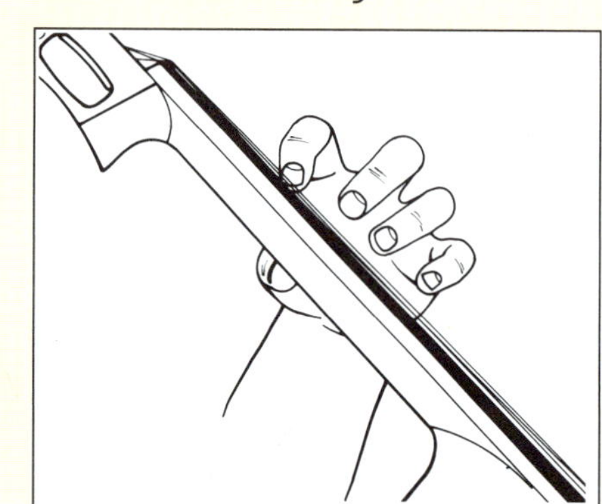

Listening Skills

Play what your teacher plays. Listen carefully.

THEORY

Ledger Lines

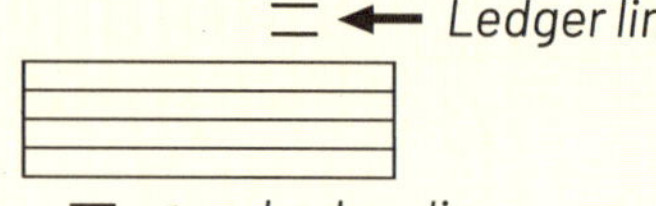

Ledger lines extend the music staff higher or lower.

23. LET'S READ "D"

D

24. LET'S READ "C♯" (C-sharp)

C♯

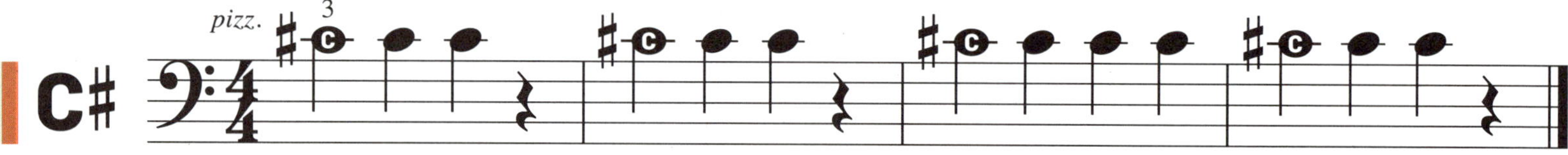

▲ *Play all C♯'s. Sharps apply to the entire measure.*

25. TAKE OFF

26. CARIBBEAN ISLAND

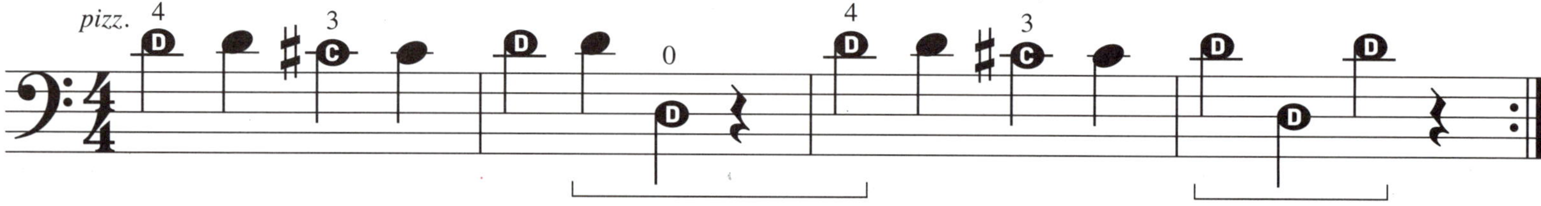

★ Practice BOW BUILDERS ONE, TWO, and THREE daily.

27. OLYMPIC HIGH JUMP

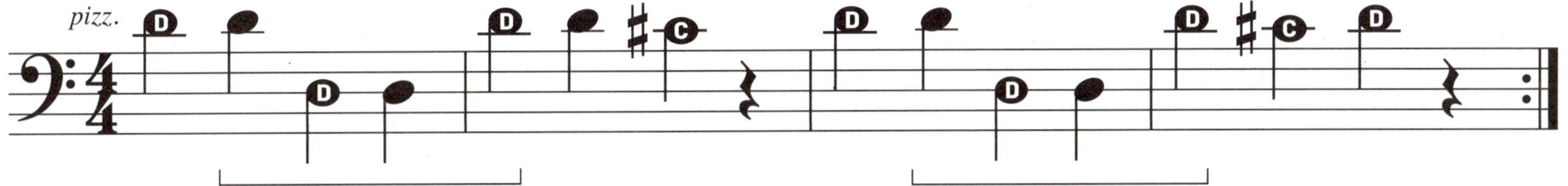

28. LET'S READ "B"

29. HALF WAY DOWN

30. RIGHT BACK UP

Scale A **scale** is a sequence of notes in ascending or descending order. Like a musical "ladder," each note is the next consecutive step of the scale. This is your D Scale. The first and last notes are both D.

THEORY

31. DOWN THE D SCALE *Remember to memorize the note names.*

32. ESSENTIAL ELEMENTS QUIZ – UP THE D SCALE

BOW BUILDER FOUR

On the Bow

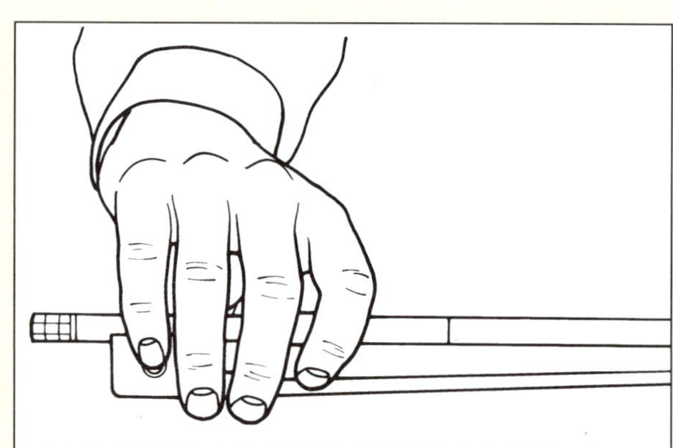

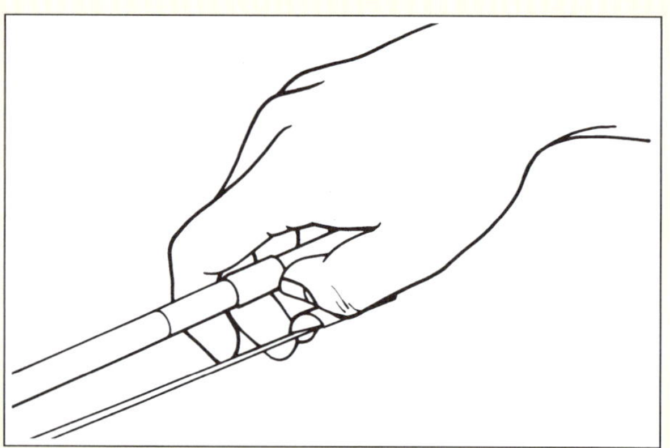

Step 1 Identify all parts of the bow (see page 2). Hold the bow in your left hand near the tip with the frog pointing to the right.

Step 2 Place the bow between your right thumb and second finger. The tip of your thumb will contact the stick next to the frog, and your second finger will extend to the ferrule.

Step 3 Shape the remaining fingers on the bow stick, as shown.

Step 4 Turn your right hand over, and be sure your thumb is curved.

Step 5 Hold the bow and repeat the exercises on page 8.

Alert Do not place your bow on the instrument until instructed to do so by your teacher.

33. SONG FOR CHRISTINE

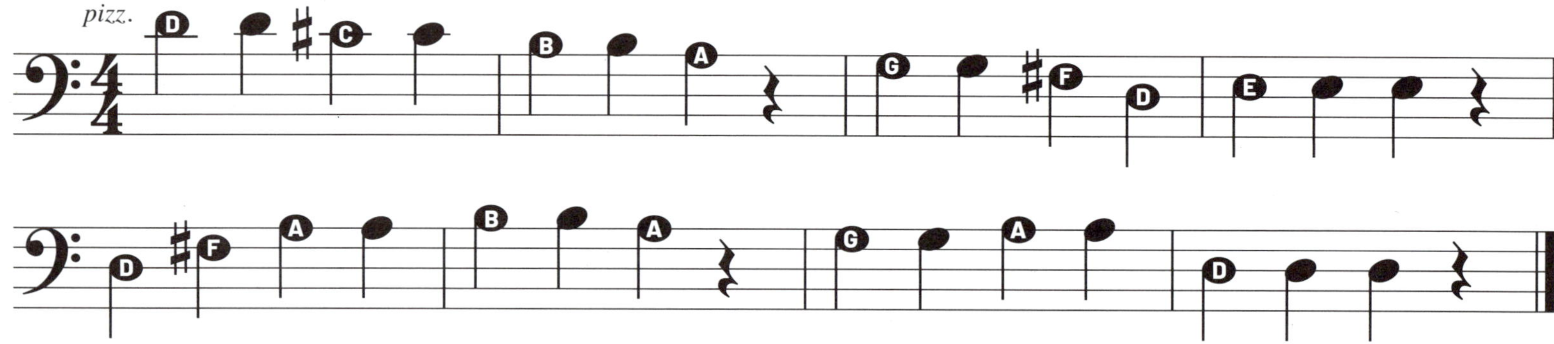

34. NATALIE'S ROSE *Remember to count.*

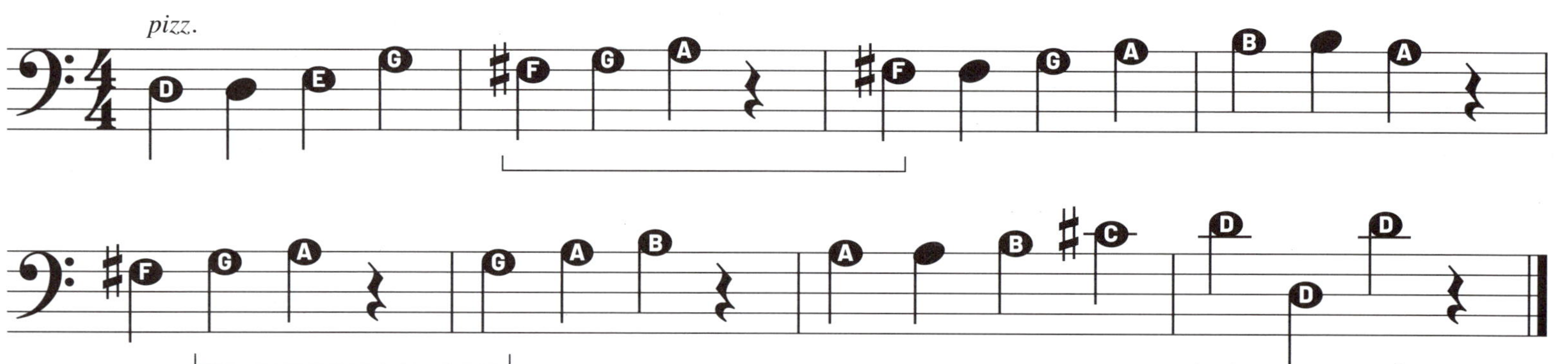

35. ESSENTIAL CREATIVITY *How many words can you create by drawing notes on the staff below?*

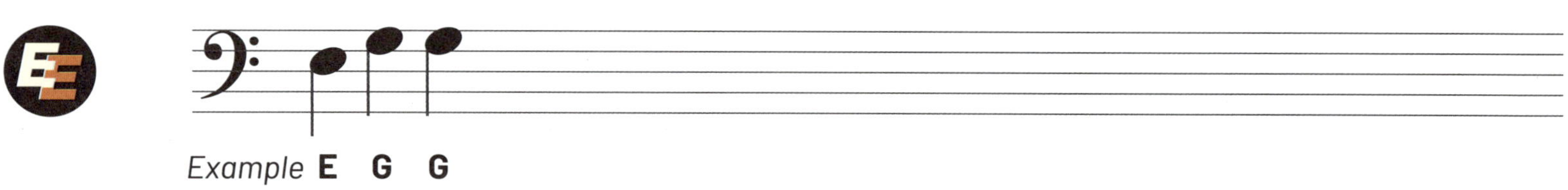

Folk songs often tell stories. This **Israeli folk song** describes a game played with a dreidel, a small table-top spinning toy that has been enjoyed by families for centuries. The game is especially popular in December around the time of Hanukkah.

36. DREIDEL

Israeli Folk Song

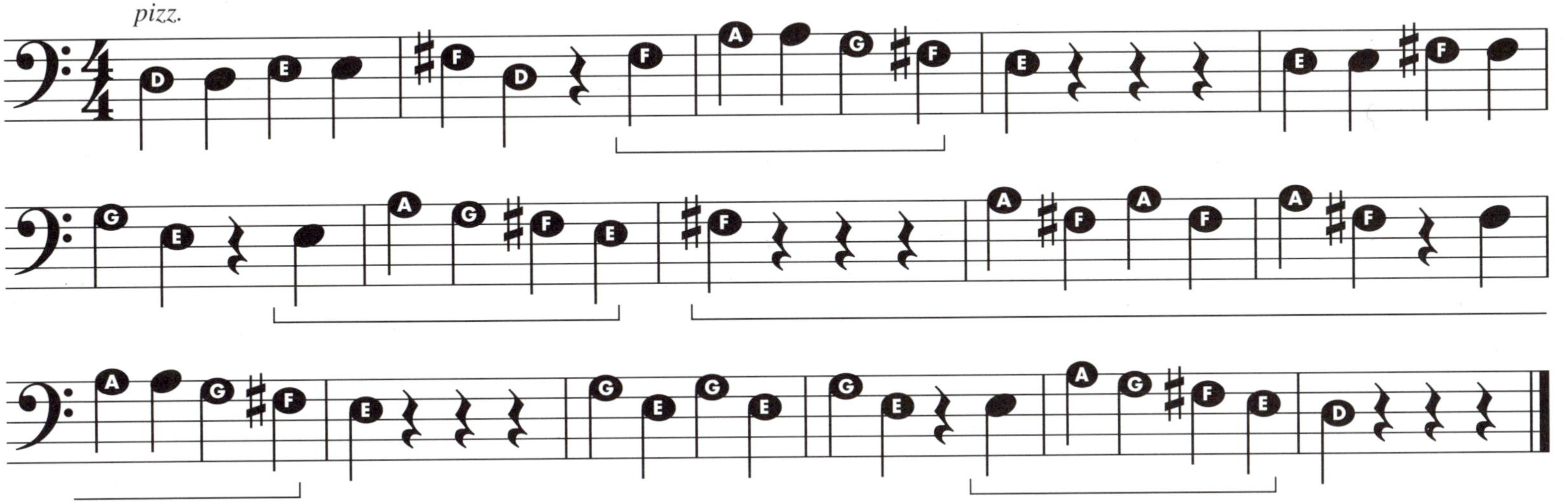

BOW BUILDER FIVE

Shadow Bowing

Shadow Bowing is bowing without the instrument.

Step 1 Tighten the bow hair as instructed by your teacher.

Step 2 Place the rosin in your left hand. Hold the bow in your right hand.

Step 3 Shadow bow by slowly moving the bow back and forth on the rosin. Be sure to move the bow, not the rosin.

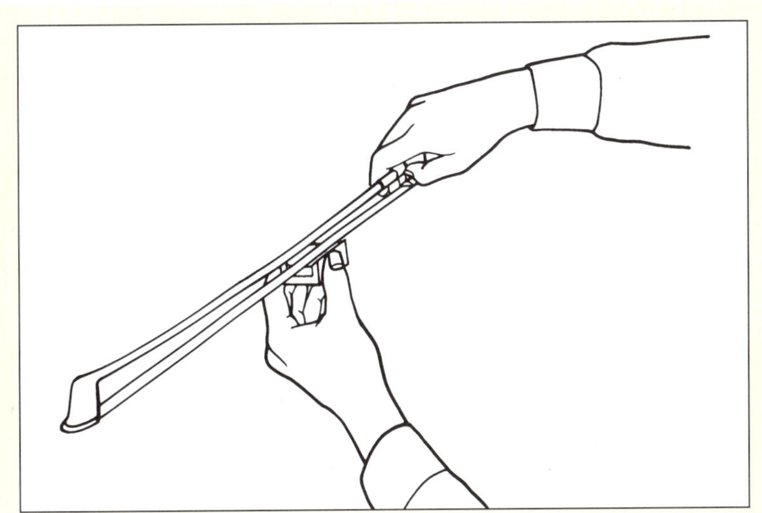

Down Bow ⊓ Move the bow away from your body (to the right).

Up Bow V Move the bow toward your body (to the left).

37. ROSIN RAP #1 *Bow these exercises on the rosin.*

38. ROSIN RAP #2

39. ROSIN RAP #3

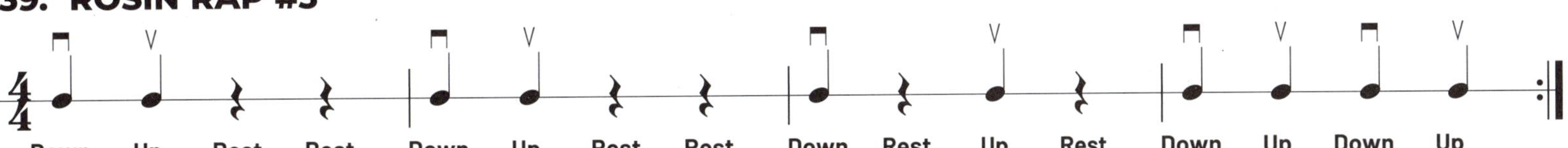

✔ Is your bow hand shaped as shown in the diagram above?

40. CAROLINA BREEZE

41. JINGLE BELLS

J. S. Pierpont

42. OLD MACDONALD HAD A FARM

American Folk Song

★ Practice BOW BUILDER FIVE daily.

HISTORY

Austrian composer **Wolfgang Amadeus Mozart** (1756–1791) was a child prodigy who first performed in concert at age 6. He lived during the time of the American Revolution (1775–1783). Mozart's music is melodic and imaginative. He wrote hundreds of compositions, including a piano piece based on this familiar song.

43. A MOZART MELODY

Adapted by W. A. Mozart

pizz.

THEORY

Key Signature D MAJOR

A **key signature** tells us what notes to play with sharps and flats throughout the entire piece. Play all F's as F♯ (F-sharp) and all C's as C♯ (C-sharp) when you see this key signature, which is called "D Major."

44. MATTHEW'S MARCH

▲ *Play F♯'s and C♯'s when you see this key signature.*

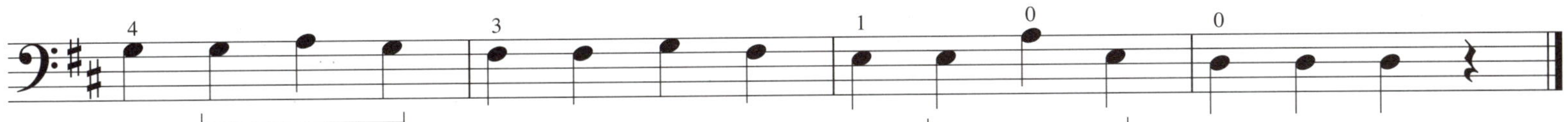

45. CHRISTOPHER'S TUNE

46. ESSENTIAL CREATIVITY

Play the notes below. Then compose your own music for the last two measures using the notes you have learned with this rhythm:

BOW BUILDER SIX

Let's Bow!

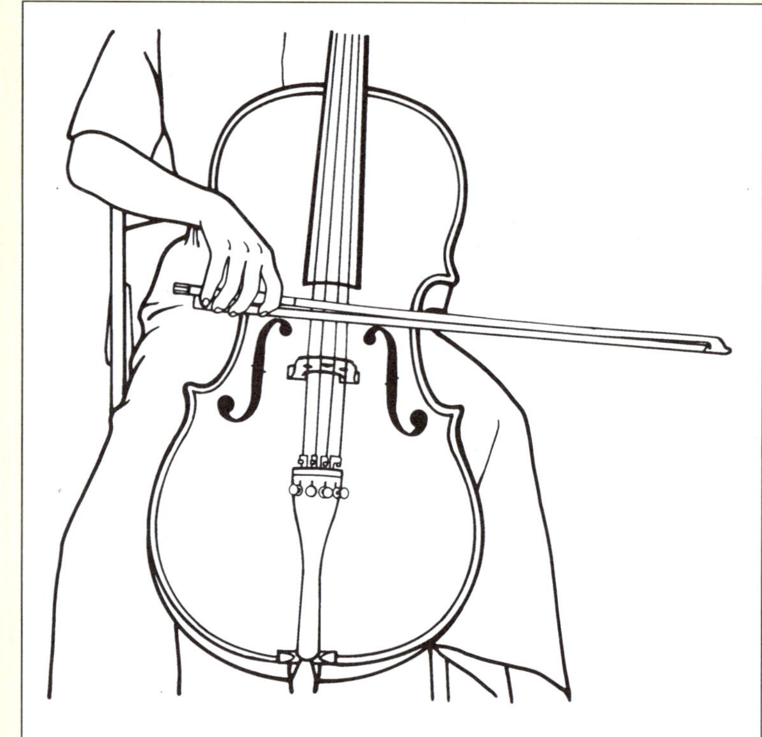

Bow Hold

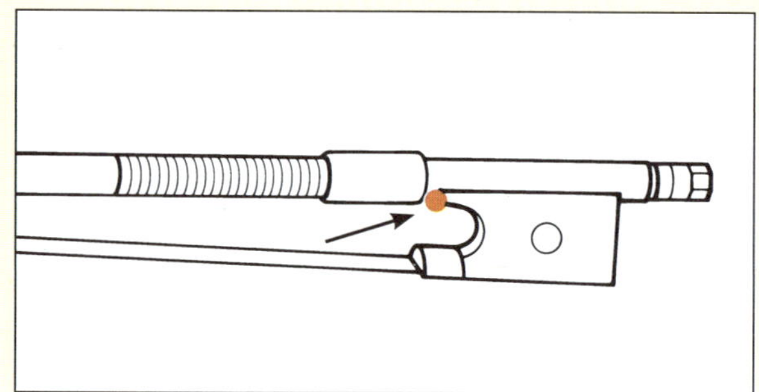

Thumb Placement

Listening Skills

Play what your teacher plays. Listen carefully. Your tone should be smooth and even.

47. BOW ON THE D STRING

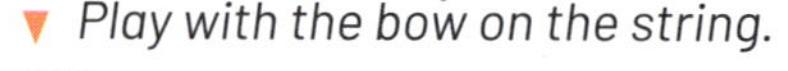

Play with the bow on the string.

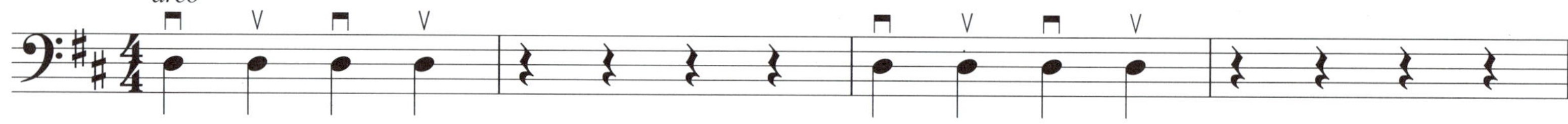

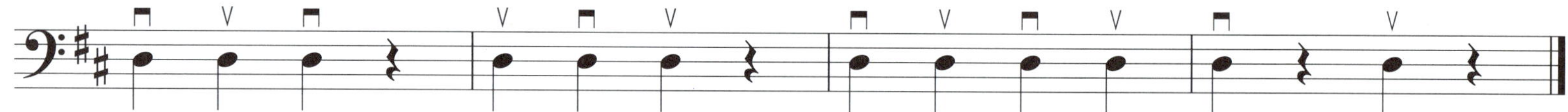

48. BOW ON THE A STRING

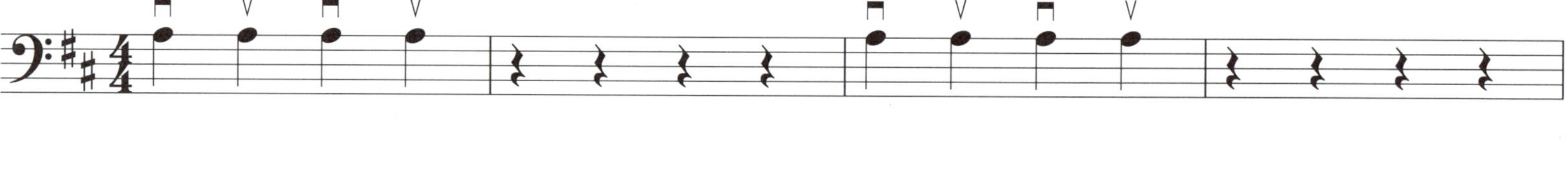

WORKOUTS

String Levels

Your arm moves when bowing on different strings. Memorize these guidelines:

- Move your arm **forward** and **up** to play **higher**-pitched strings.
- Move your arm **back** and **down** to play **lower**-pitched strings.

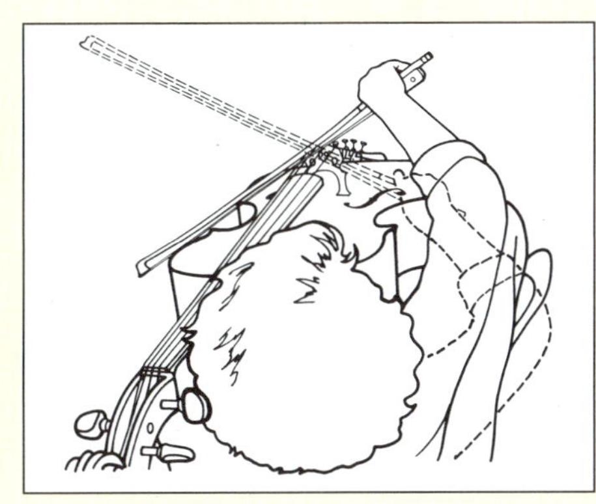

Raise arm = higher string

Lower arm = lower string

49. RAISE AND LOWER

50. TEETER TOTTER

51. MIRROR IMAGE

Bow Lift

, Lift the bow and return to its starting point.

52. A STRAND OF D 'N' A

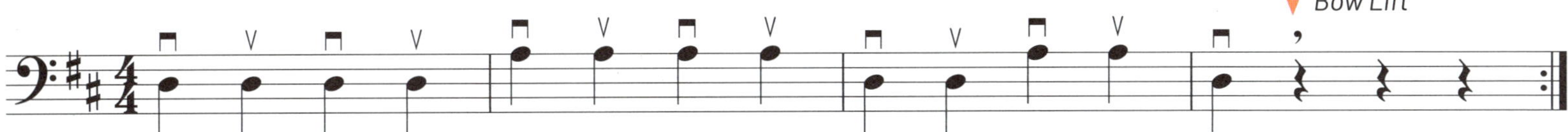

53. ESSENTIAL ELEMENTS QUIZ – OLYMPIC CHALLENGE

BOW BUILDER SEVEN

Combining Both Hands

Using notes from the D major scale, echo what your teacher plays.

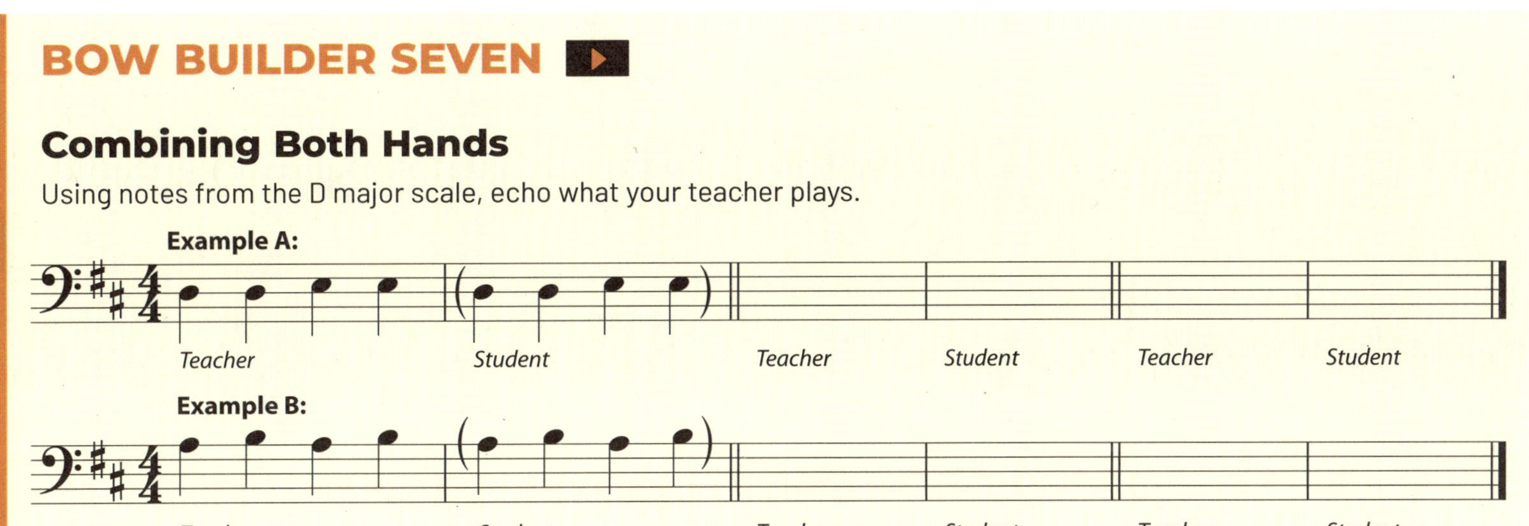

PUTTING IT ALL TOGETHER

Congratulations! You are now ready to practice like an advanced player by combining left and right hand skills while reading music. When learning a new line of music, follow these steps for success:

 **Step 1** Tap your toe and say or sing the letter names.

Step 2 Play *pizz.* and say or sing the letter names.

Step 3 Shadow bow and say or sing the letter names.

Step 4 Bow and play as written.

54. BOWING "G"

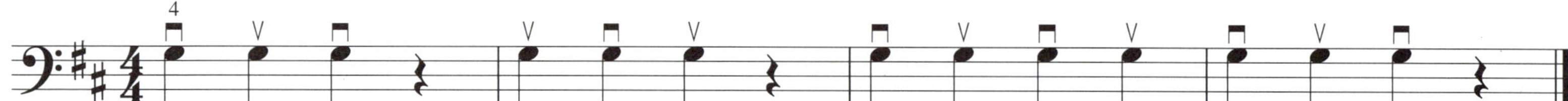

55. BACK AND FORTH

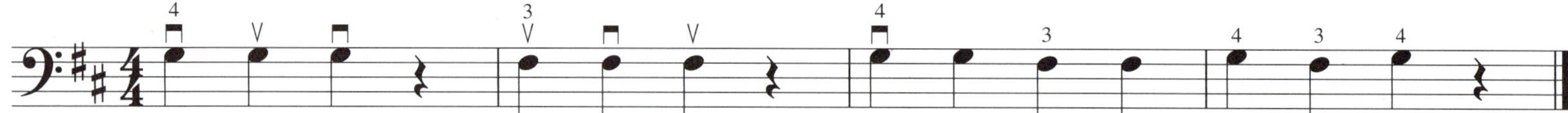

56. DOWN AND UP

57. TRIBAL LAMENT

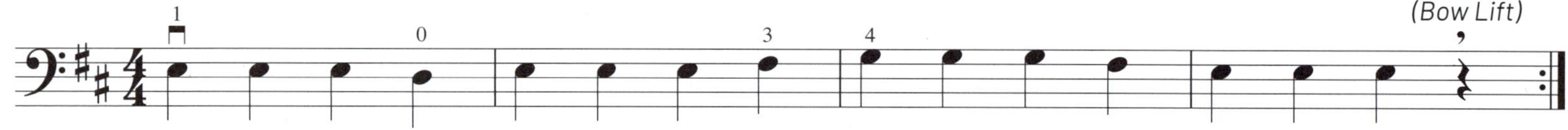

58. BOWING "D"

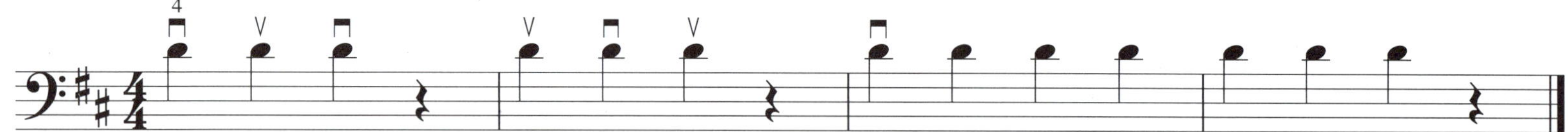

59. LITTLE STEPS

60. ELEVATOR DOWN

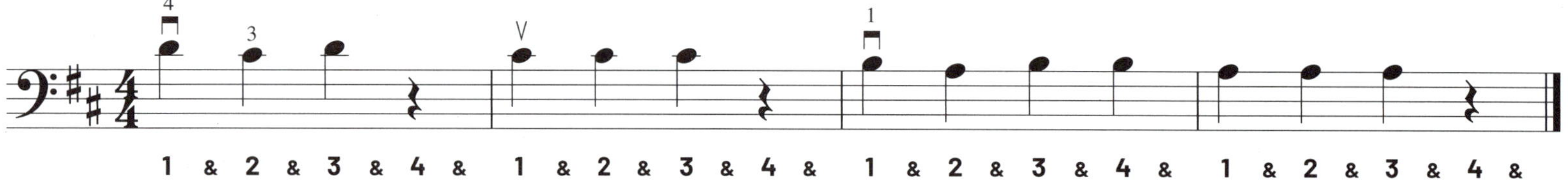

61. ELEVATOR UP

62. DOWN THE D MAJOR SCALE

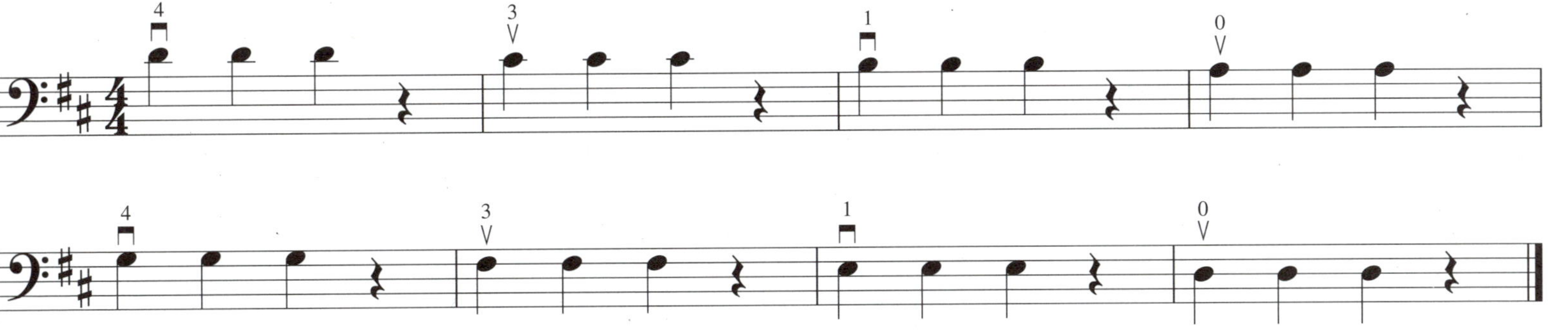

63. SCALE SIMULATOR *Remember to count.*

64. ESSENTIAL ELEMENTS QUIZ – THE D MAJOR SCALE

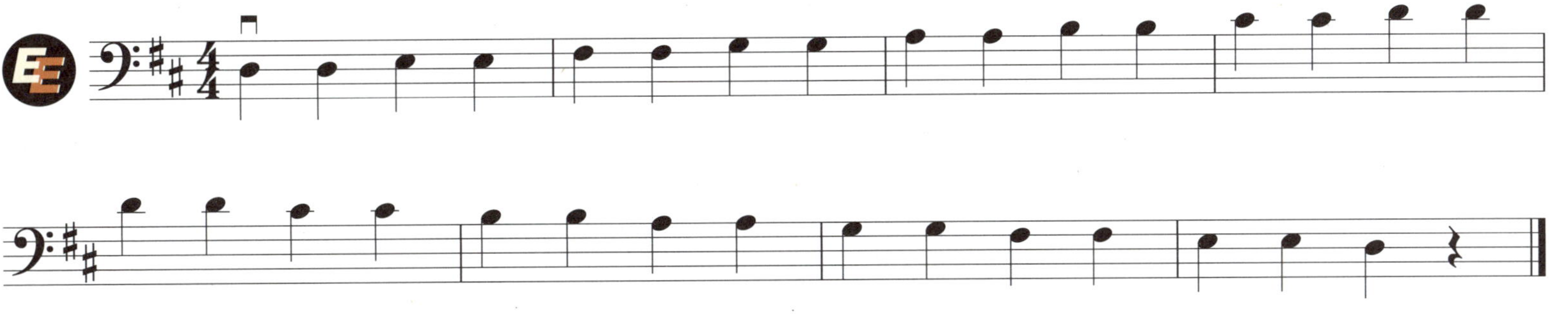

Special Cello Exercise

While the basses learn a new note, draw the bar lines in the music below. Then write in the counting.

65. LET'S READ "C♯" – Review

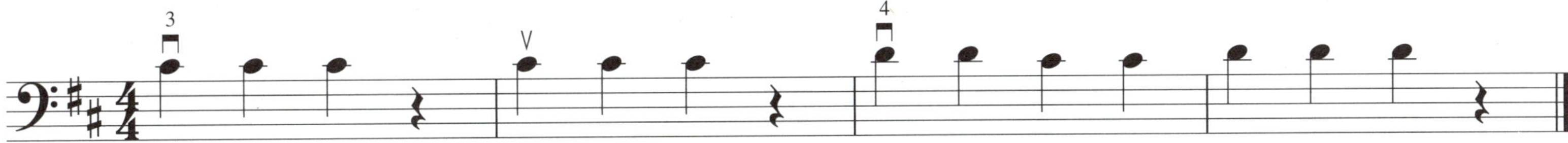

THEORY

Eighth Notes

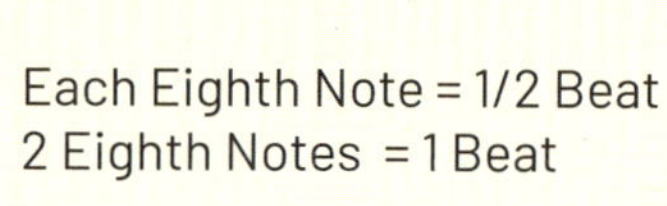

Each Eighth Note = 1/2 Beat
2 Eighth Notes = 1 Beat

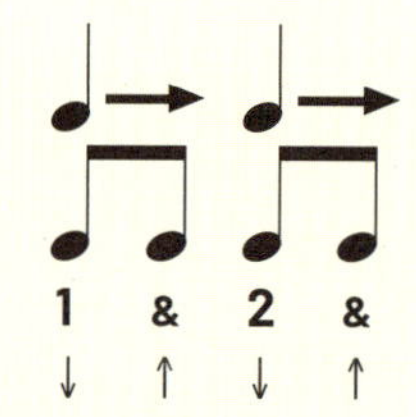

Two or more Eighth Notes have a *beam* across the stems.

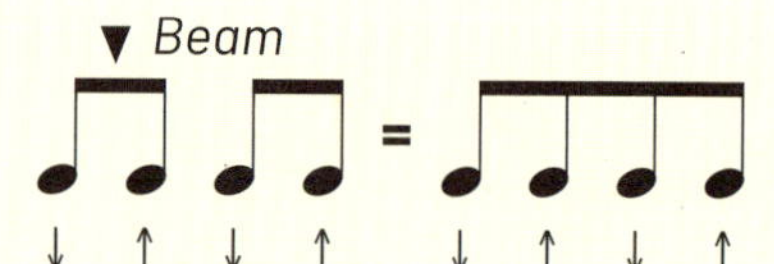

Tap your toe down on the number and up on the "&."

66. RHYTHM RAP

Shadow bow and count before playing.

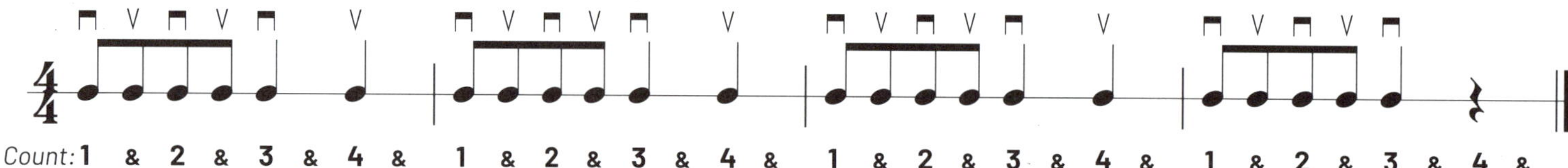

67. PEPPERONI PIZZA

68. RHYTHM RAP

Shadow bow and count before playing.

69. D MAJOR SCALE UP

Tempo Markings

Tempo is the speed of music. Tempo markings are usually written above the staff, in Italian.

Allegro – Fast tempo **Moderato** – Medium tempo **Andante** – Slower, walking tempo

70. HOT CROSS BUNS

Moderato

71. AU CLAIRE DE LA LUNE

French Folk Song

Andante

72. RHYTHM RAP

Shadow bow and count before playing.

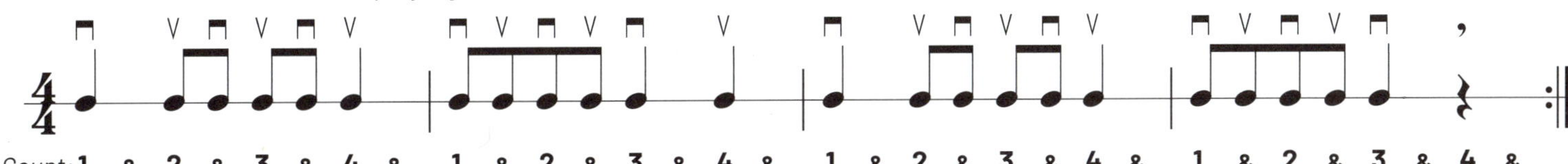

73. BUCKEYE SALUTE

Moderato

2/4 Time Signature

= **2 beats** per measure
= **Quarter** note gets one beat

Conducting

Practice conducting this two-beat pattern.

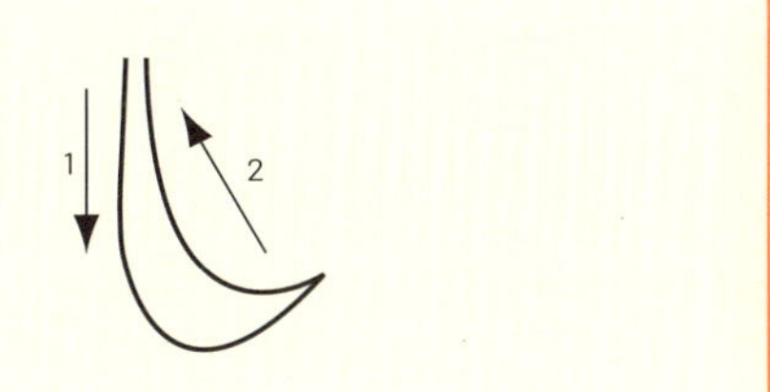

THEORY

74. RHYTHM RAP

Shadow bow and count before playing.

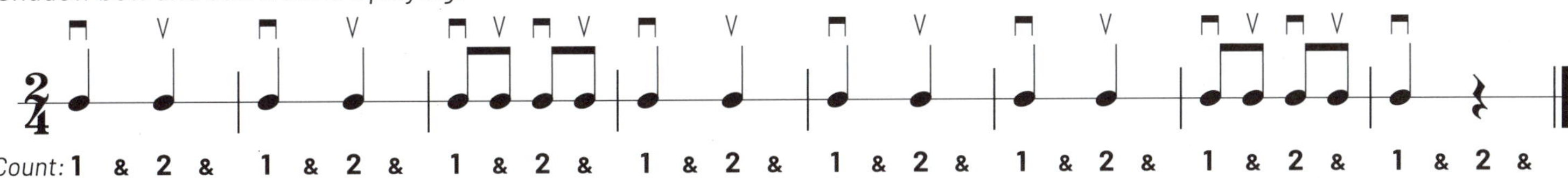

75. TWO BY TWO

1st & 2nd Endings

Play the 1st ending the 1st time through. Then, repeat the same section of music, skip the 1st ending, and play the 2nd ending.

THEORY

76. ESSENTIAL ELEMENTS QUIZ – FOR PETE'S SAKE

Moderato

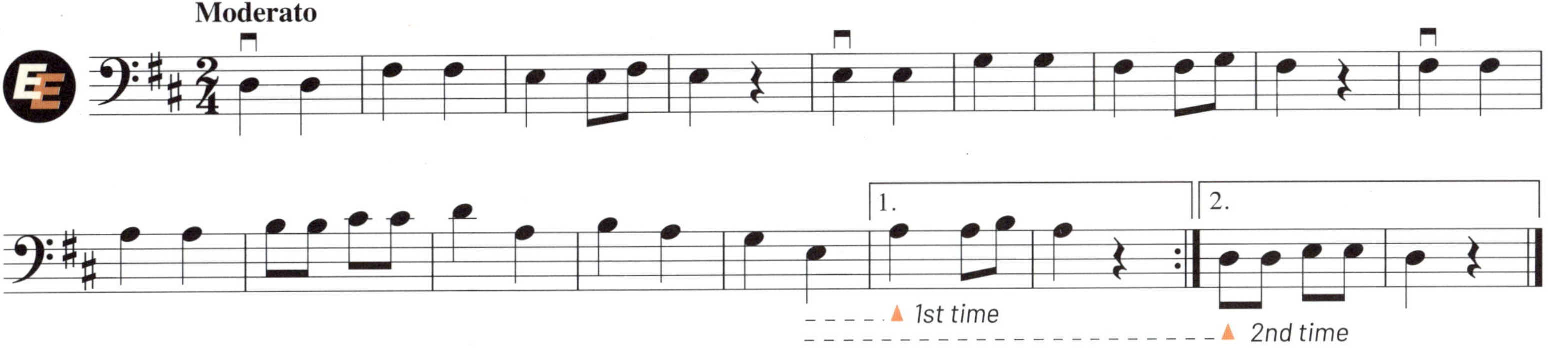

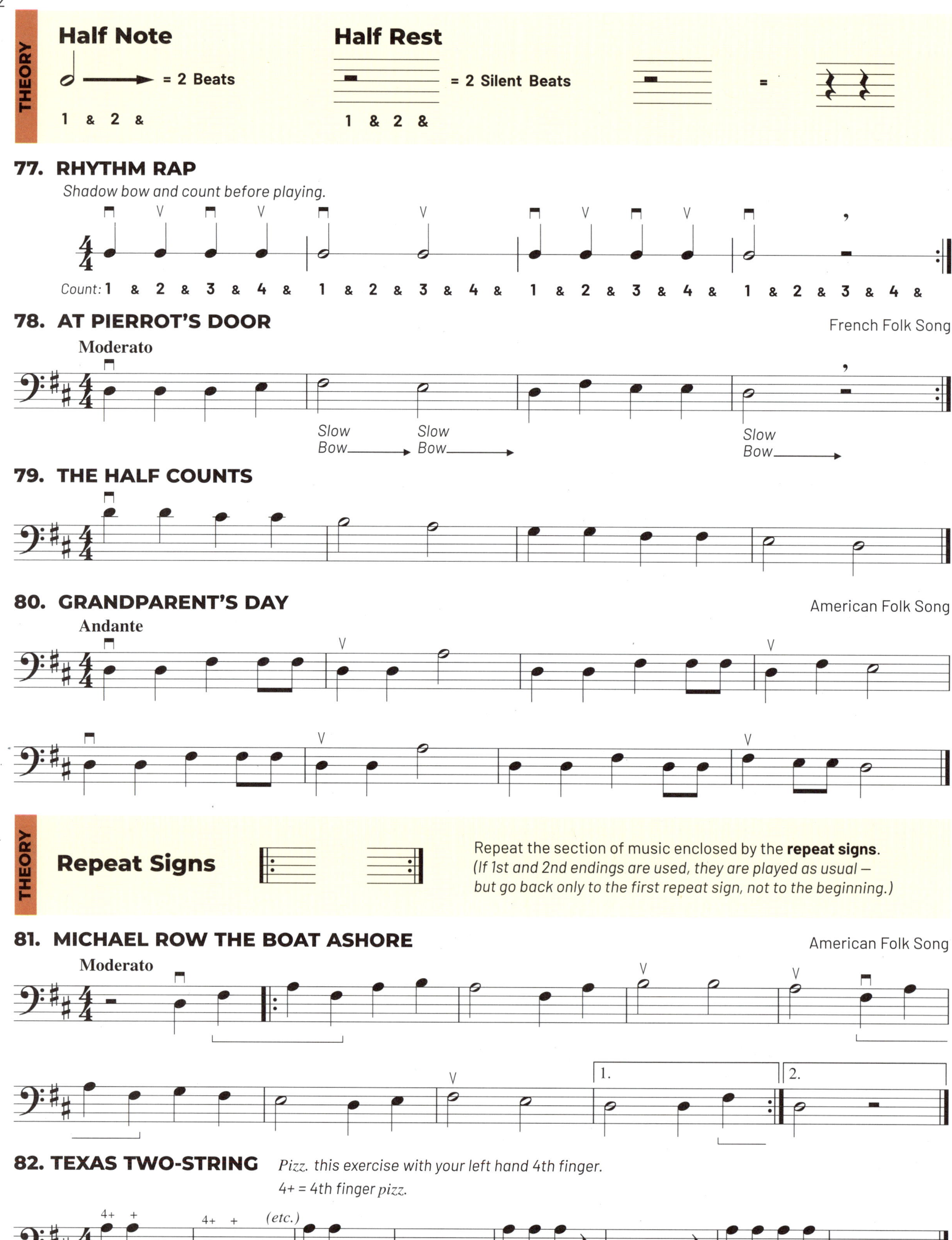

Looking for some more fun music to play?
See the inside front cover for instructions on accessing recent popular Bonus Songs.

83. FOUR BY FOUR

84. 4TH FINGER MARATHON

85. HIGH FLYING

HISTORY

German composer **Ludwig van Beethoven** (1770–1827) was one of the world's greatest composers. He was completely deaf by 1802. Although he could not hear music like we do, he could "hear" it in his mind. The theme of his final *Symphony No. 9* is called "Ode To Joy," and was written to the text of a poem by Friedrich von Schiller. "Ode To Joy" was featured in concerts celebrating the reunification of Germany in 1990.

86. ESSENTIAL ELEMENTS QUIZ – ODE TO JOY

Ludwig van Beethoven

PERFORMANCE SPOTLIGHT

 Good performers are on time with their instruments and music ready, dressed appropriately, and know their music well.

87. SCALE WARM-UP

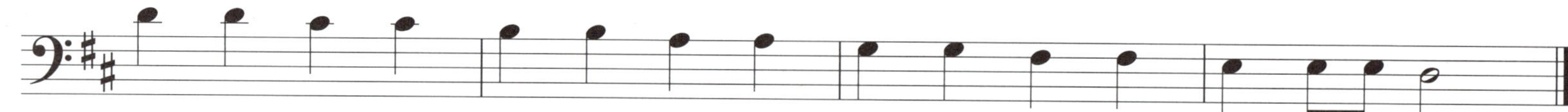

88. FRÈRE JACQUES – Round *(When group A reaches ②, group B begins at ①)*

French Folk Song

Moderato

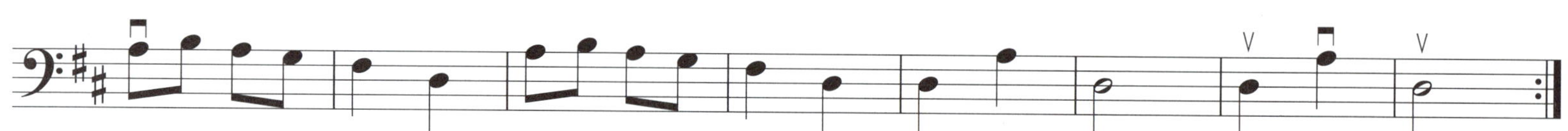

THEORY

Chord, Harmony

Two or more pitches sounding at the same time form a **chord** or **harmony**. Throughout this book, **A** = Melody and **B** = Harmony.

89. BOIL 'EM CABBAGE DOWN – Orchestra Arrangement

American Fiddle Tune

Allegro

5 ◄ *Measure Number*

PERFORMANCE SPOTLIGHT

90. ENGLISH ROUND

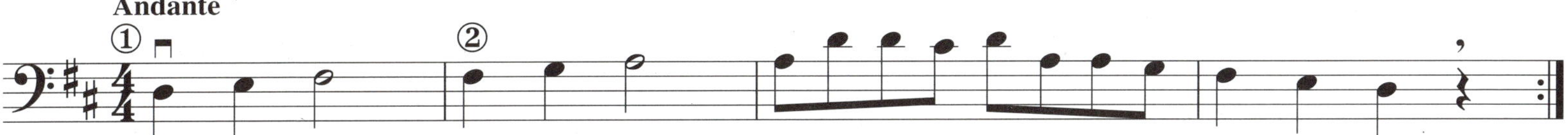

91. LIGHTLY ROW – Orchestra Arrangement

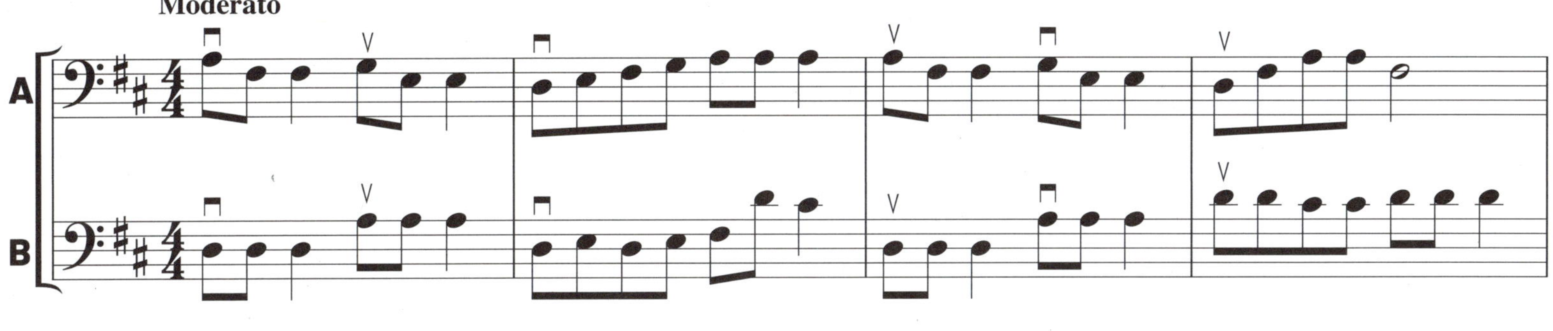

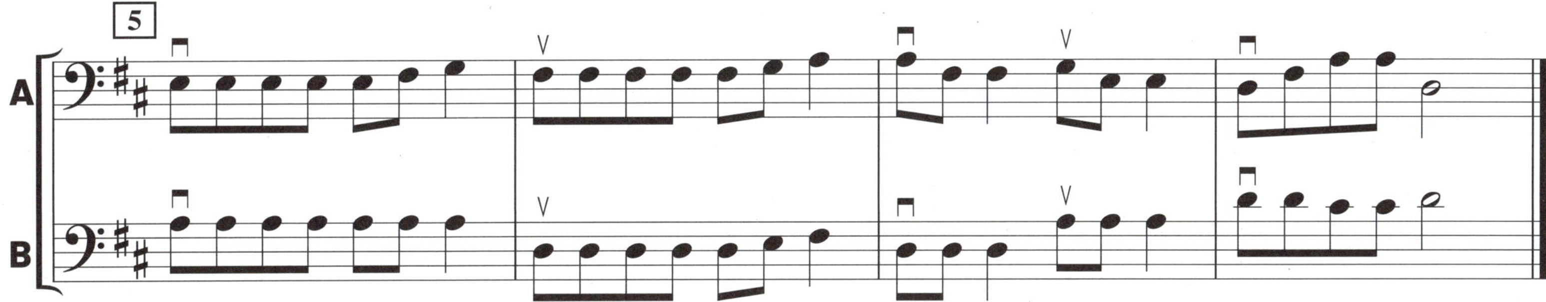

French composer **Jacques Offenbach** (1819–1880) was the originator of the **operetta** and played the cello. An **operetta** is a form of entertainment that combines several of the fine arts together: vocal and instrumental music, drama, dance, and visual arts. One of his most famous pieces is the "Can-Can" dance from *Orpheus And The Underworld*. This popular work was written in 1858, just three years before the start of the American Civil War (1861–1865).

HISTORY

92. CAN-CAN – Orchestra Arrangement

Jacques Offenbach
Arr. John Higgins

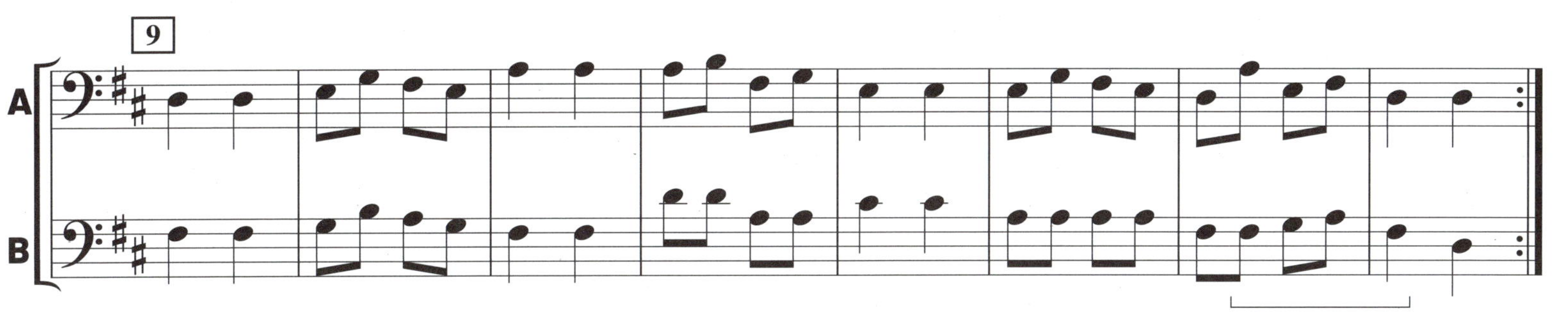

✔ What were the strong points of your performance?

G STRING NOTES

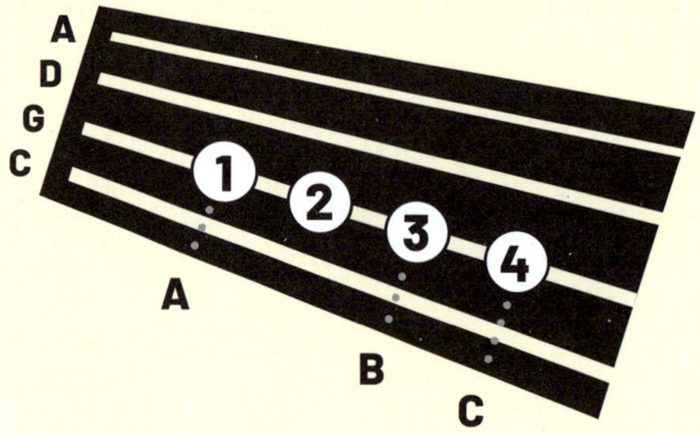

C is played with 4 fingers on the G string.

B is played with 3 fingers on the G string.

A is played with 1 finger on the G string.

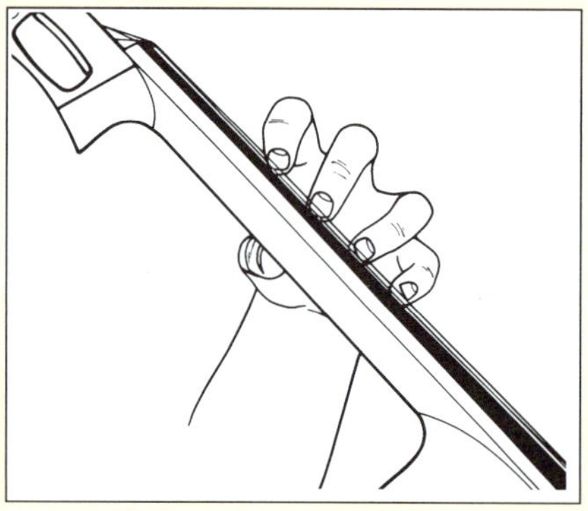

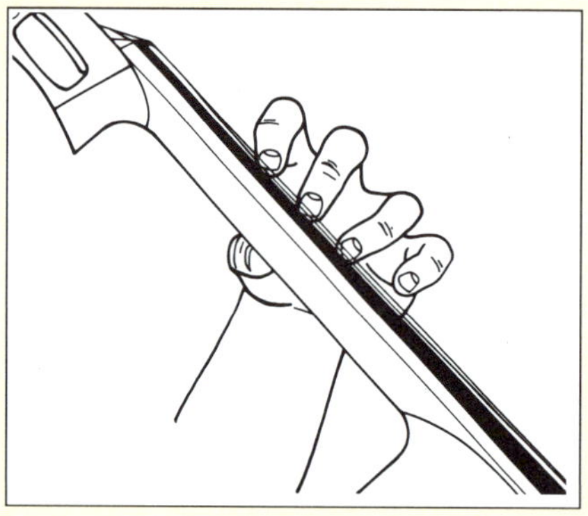

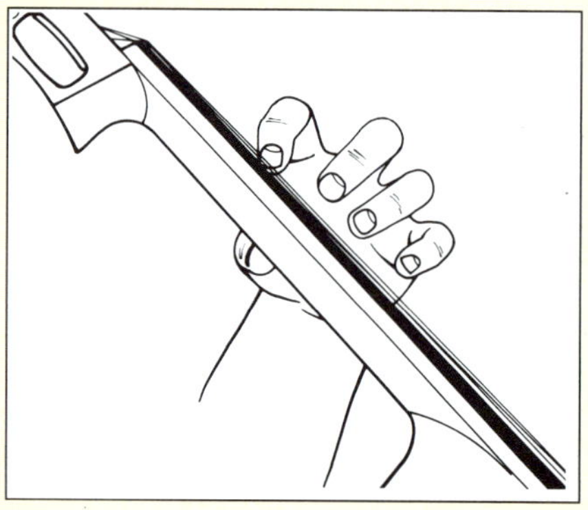

Listening Skills Play what your teacher plays. Listen carefully.

THEORY

Key Signature
G MAJOR

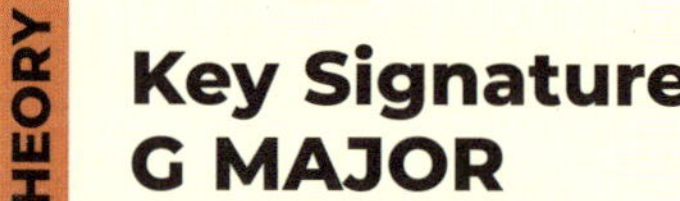

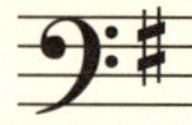

Play all F's as F♯ (F-sharp) and all C's as C♮ (C-natural).

93. LET'S READ "G"

G

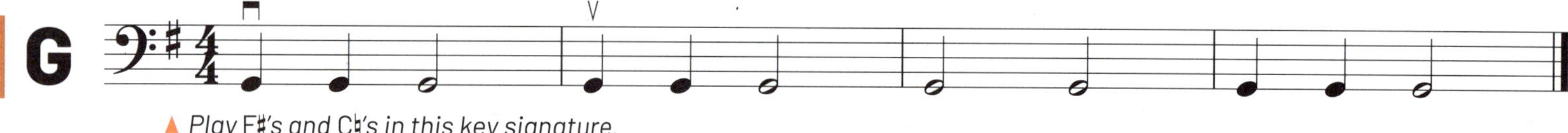

▲ *Play F♯'s and C♮'s in this key signature.*

94. LET'S READ "C" (C-natural)

C

95. LET'S READ "B"

B

96. LET'S READ "A"

A

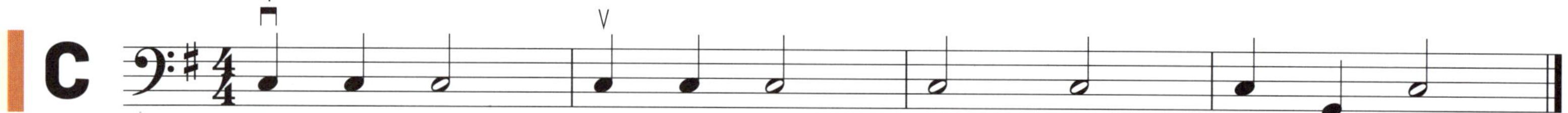

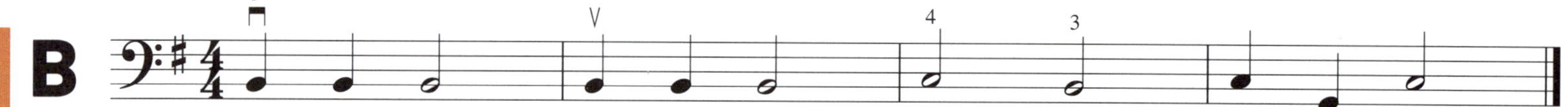

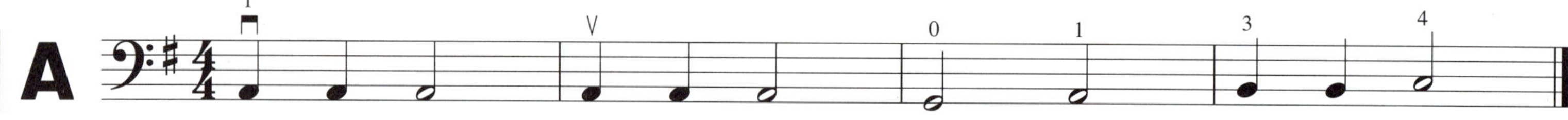

97. WALKING AROUND *Name the notes before you play.*

98. G MAJOR SCALE *Write the note names before you play.*

99. FOURTH FINGER D *(for violins and violas)*

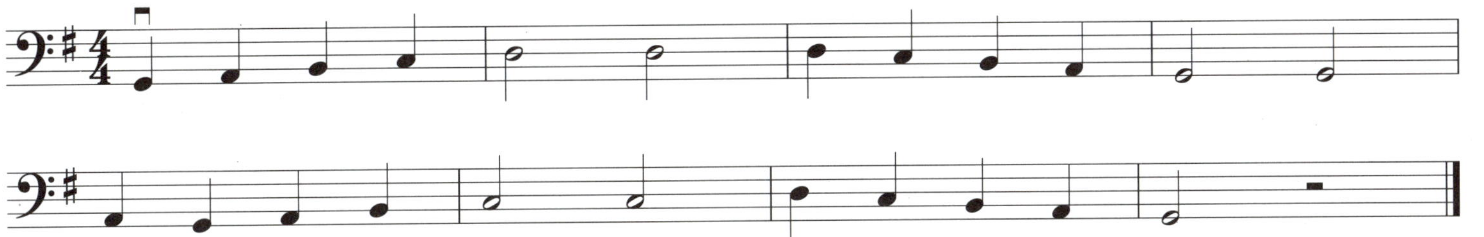

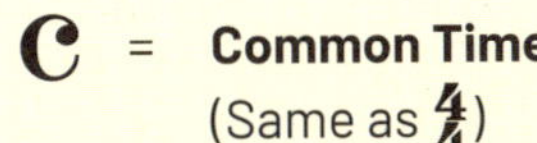

Conducting

Practice conducting this four-beat pattern.

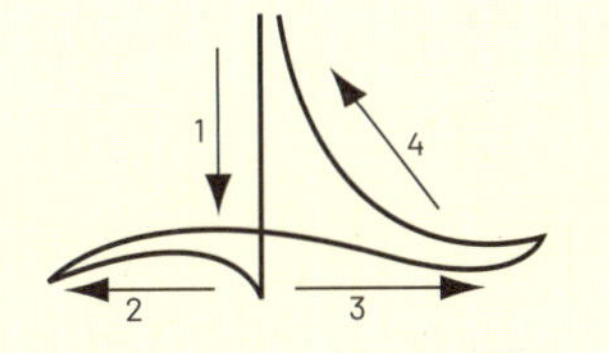

THEORY

100. LOW DOWN

101. BAA BAA BLACK SHEEP

102. ESSENTIAL ELEMENTS QUIZ – THIS OLD MAN

American Folk Song

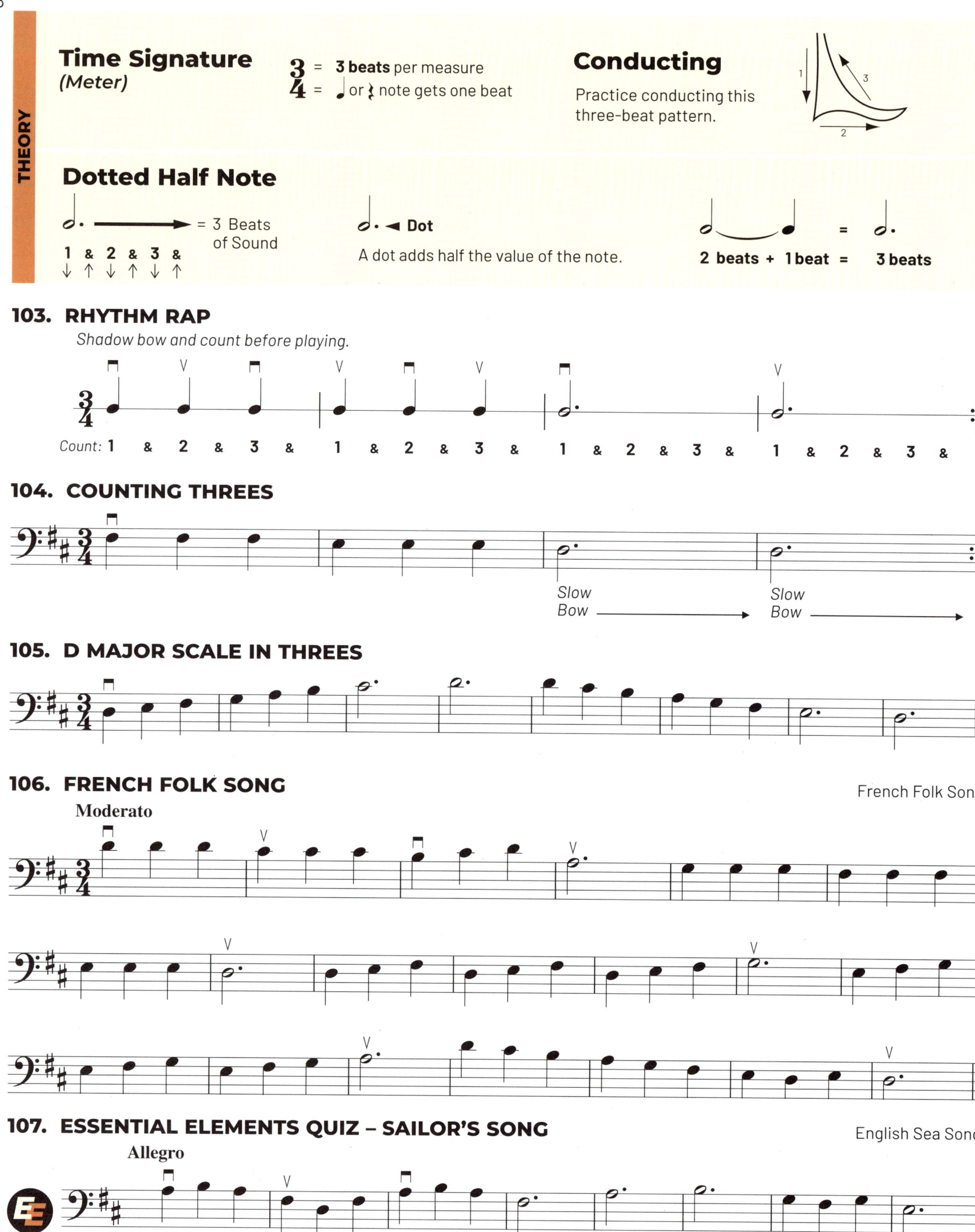

▲ *Write in the correct time signature before you begin.*

Tie

A **tie** is a curved line that connects notes of the **same** pitch.
Play a single note for the combined counts of the tied notes.

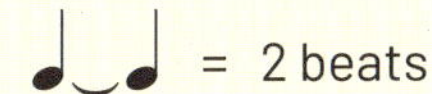

108. FIT TO BE TIED

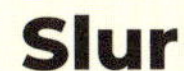

Slur

A **slur** is a curved line that connects two or more **different** pitches.
Play slurred notes together in the same bow stroke.

THEORY

109. STOP AND GO

110. SLURRING ALONG

111. SMOOTH SAILING

112. D MAJOR SLURS

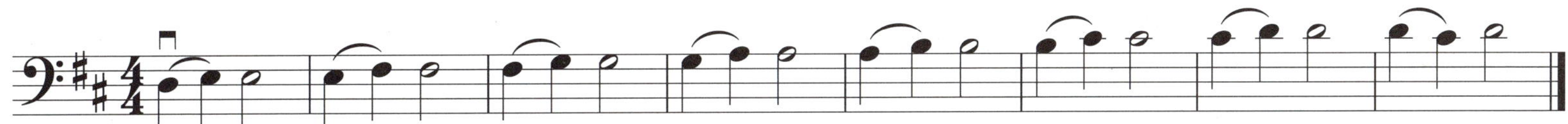

113. CROSSING STRINGS

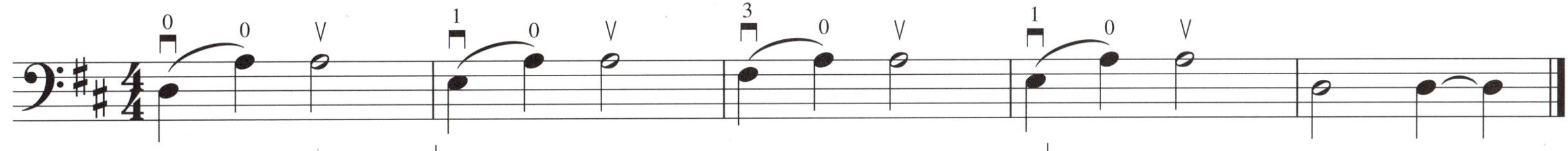

114. GLIDING BOWS

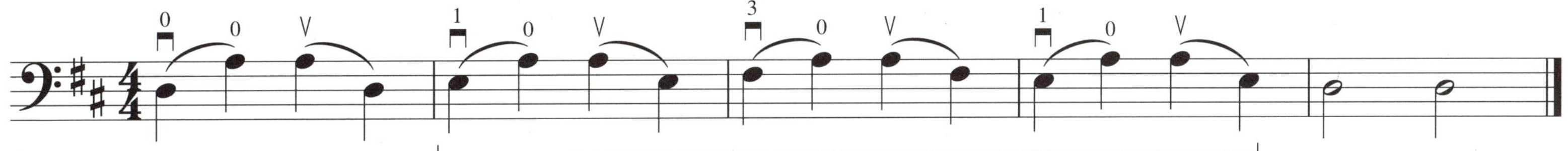

115. UPSIDE DOWN

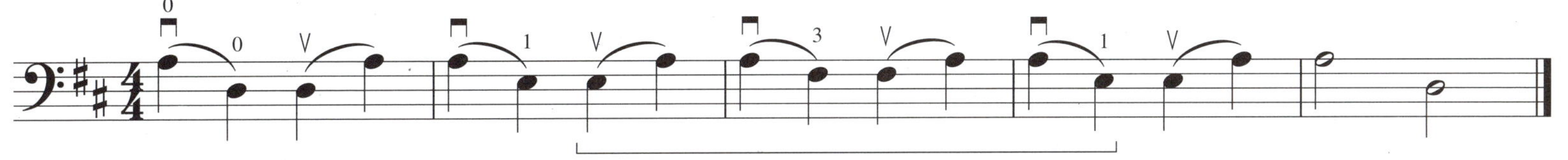

Upbeat

A note (or notes) that appears before the first full measure is called an **upbeat** (or **pickup**). The remaining beats are found in the last measure.

116. SONG FOR MARIA

HISTORY

Latin American music combines the folk music from South and Central America, the Caribbean Islands, African, Spanish, and Portuguese cultures. Melodies often feature a lively accompaniment by drums, maracas, and claves. Latin American styles have become part of jazz, classical, and rock music.

THEORY

D.C. al Fine

Play until you see the **D.C. al Fine**. Then go back to the beginning and play until you see **Fine** (*fee'- nay*). **D.C.** is the abbreviation for **Da Capo**, the Italian term for "return to the beginning." **Fine** is the Italian word for "the finish."

117. BANANA BOAT SONG

Caribbean Folk Song

118. FIROLIRALERA – Orchestra Arrangement

Mexican Folk Song
Arr. John Higgins

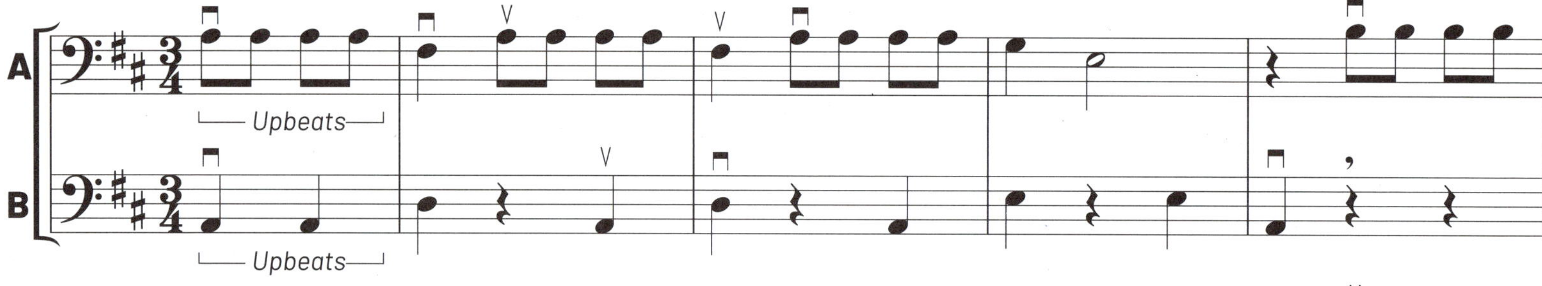

SKILL BUILDERS – G Major

119.

120.

121.

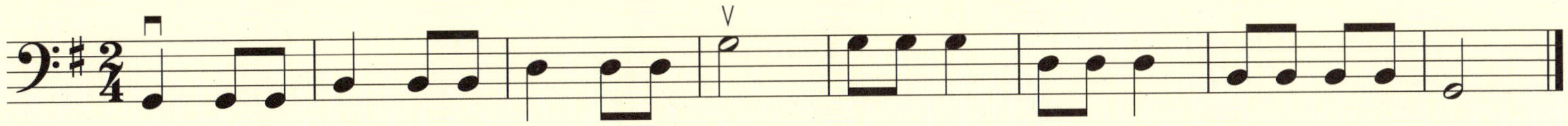

122.

123.

Slur three

124.

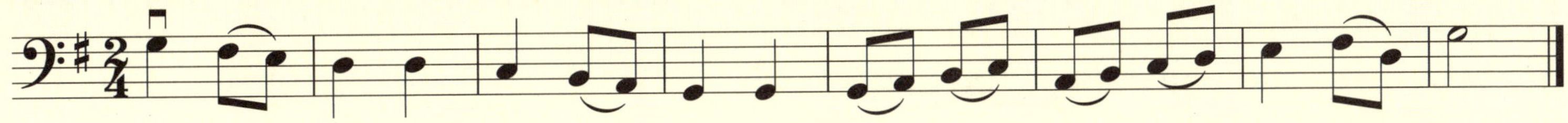

HISTORY

Far Eastern music comes from Malaysia, Indonesia, China and other areas. Historians believe the first orchestras, known as **gamelans**, existed in this region as early as the 1st century B.C. Today's gamelans include rebabs (spiked fiddles), gongs, xylophones, and a wide variety of percussion instruments.

125. JINGLI NONA

Far Eastern Folk Song

Second Finger on the D String

F

is played with 2 fingers on the D string.

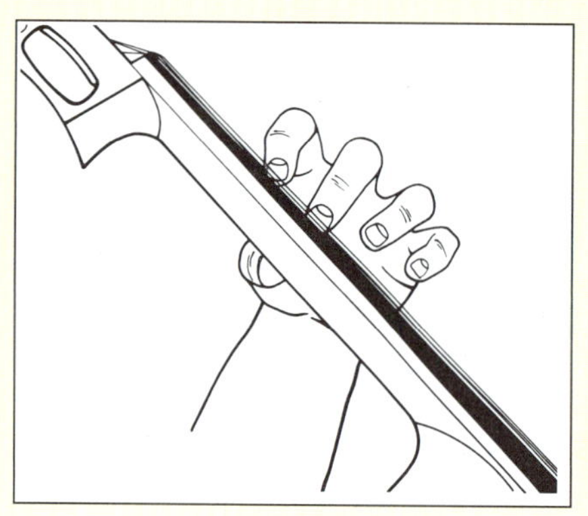

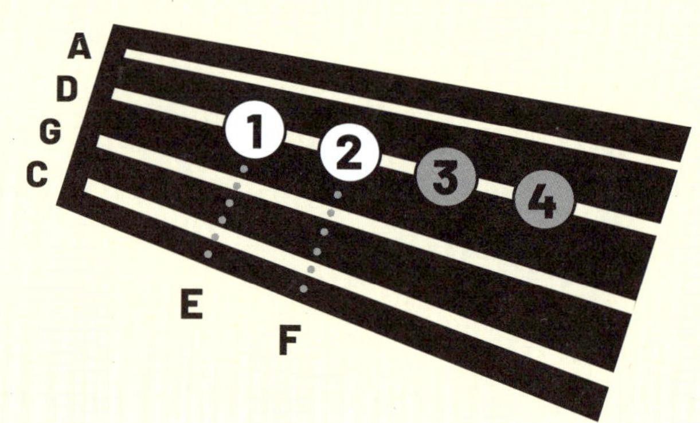

Listening Skills

Play what your teacher plays. Listen carefully.

THEORY

Natural ♮

A **natural** sign cancels out a flat (♭) or a sharp (♯) and remains in effect for the entire measure.

126. LET'S READ "F" (F-natural)

THEORY

Half Step
Whole Step

A **half step** is the smallest distance between two notes.

A **whole step** is two half steps combined.

127. HALF-STEPPIN' AND WHOLE-STEPPIN'

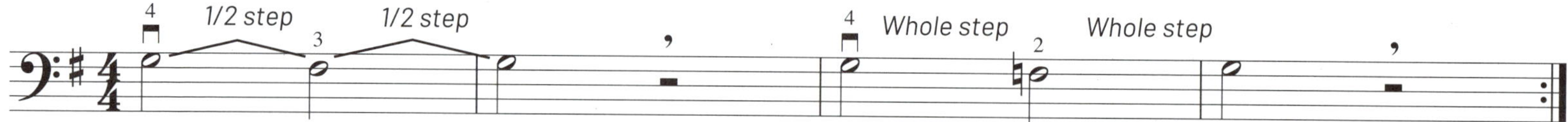

128. SPY GUY

129. MINOR DETAILS

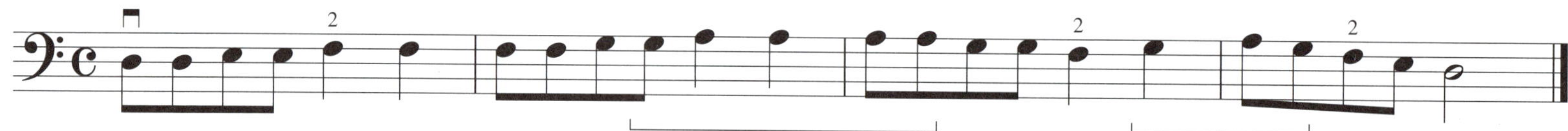

Second Finger on the A String

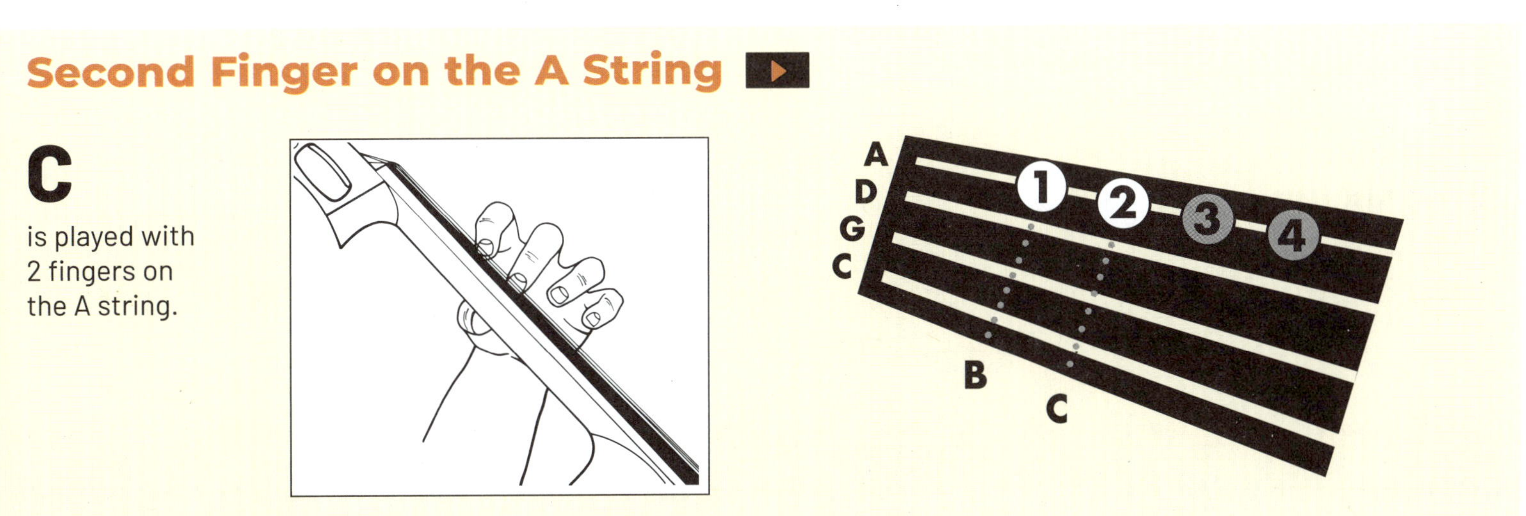

Listening Skills Play what your teacher plays. Listen carefully.

130. LET'S READ "C" (C-natural)

131. HALF STEP AND WHOLE STEP REVIEW

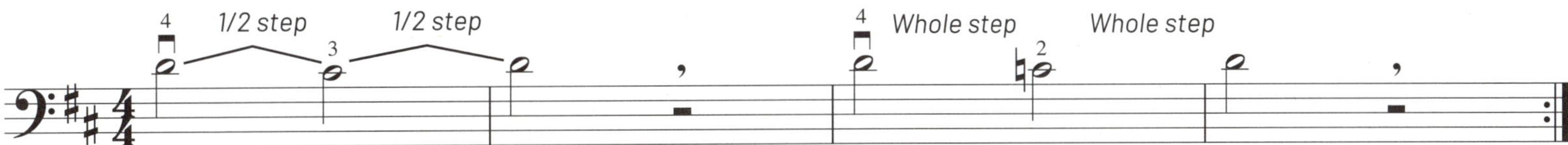

Chromatics — **Chromatic notes** are altered with sharps, flats, and naturals.
A chromatic pattern is two or more notes in a sequence of half steps.

THEORY

132. CHROMATIC MOVES

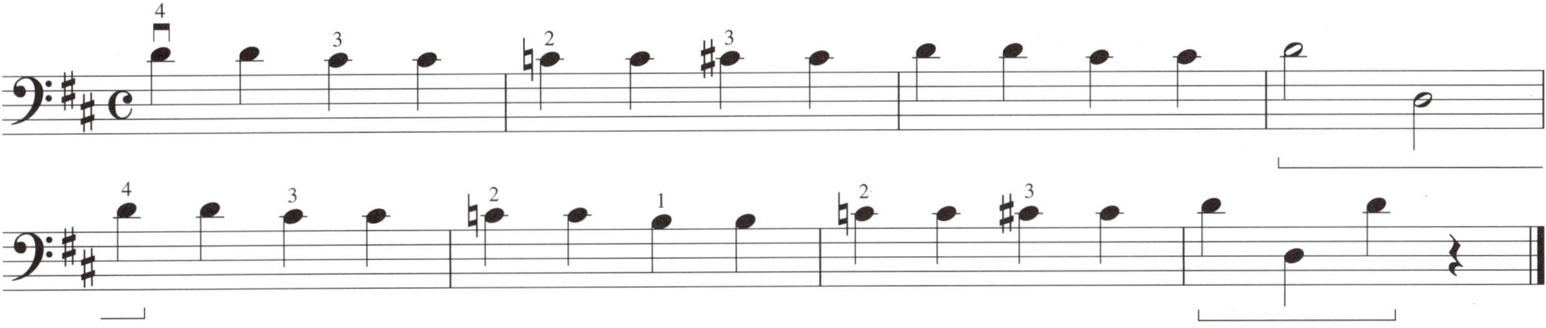

133. THE STETSON SPECIAL

134. BLUEBIRD'S SONG

Texas Folk Song

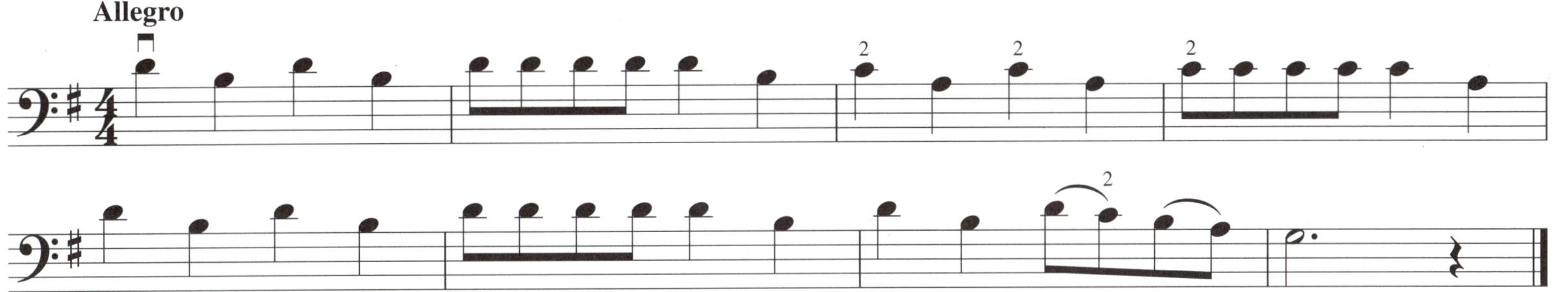

THEORY

Key Signature C MAJOR — All notes are naturals.

135. C MAJOR SCALE – Round

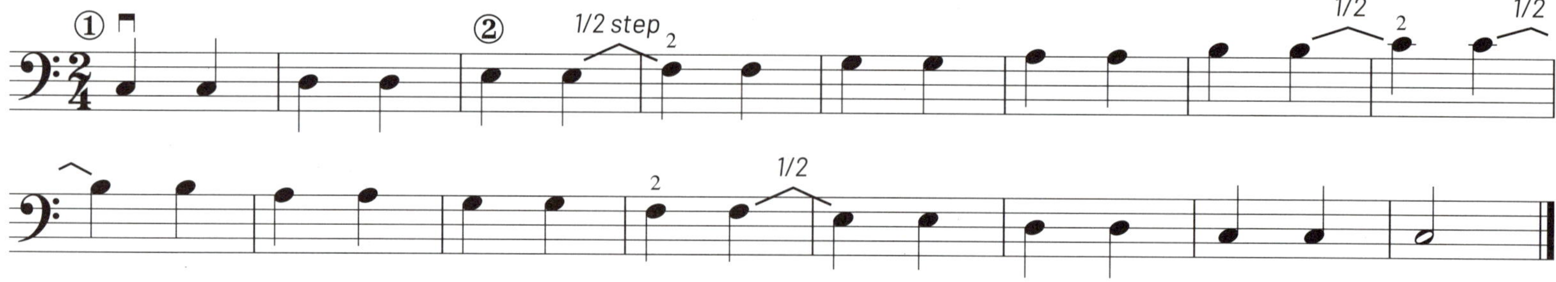

Duet — A composition with two different parts, played together.

136. SPLIT DECISION – Duet

137. OAK HOLLOW

Moderato

138. A-TISKET, A-TASKET

Allegro

HISTORY

In the second half of the 1800s many composers tried to express the spirit of their own country by writing music with a distinct national flavor. Listen to the music of Russian composers such as Borodin, Tchaikovsky, and Rimsky-Korsakov. They often used folk songs and dance rhythms to convey their nationalism. Describe the sounds you hear.

139. ESSENTIAL ELEMENTS QUIZ – RUSSIAN FOLK TUNE

Russian Folk Song

Andante

Alert This page mixes finger patterns. Watch for 2nd finger (C♮) and 3rd finger (F♯).

140. BINGO

18th Century English Game Song

Where is beat 2? ▲

HISTORY

English composer **Thomas Tallis** (1505–1585) served as royal court composer during the reigns of Henry VIII, Edward VI, Mary, and Elizabeth I. Composers and artists during this era wanted to recreate the artistic and scientific glories of ancient Greece and Rome. The great artist Michelangelo painted the Sistine Chapel during Tallis' lifetime. **Rounds** and **canons** were popular forms of music during the early 16th century. Divide into groups, and play or sing the *Tallis Canon* as a 4-part round.

141. TALLIS CANON – Round

Thomas Tallis

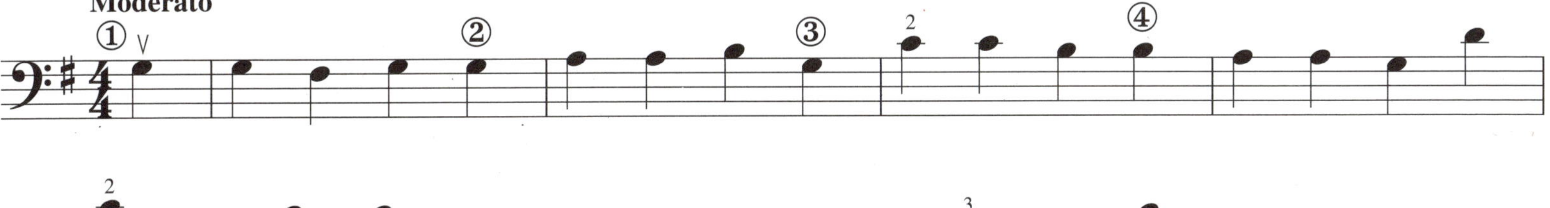

THEORY

Theme and Variations

Theme and Variations is a musical form where a theme, or melody, is followed by different versions of the same theme.

142. VARIATIONS ON A FAMILIAR SONG

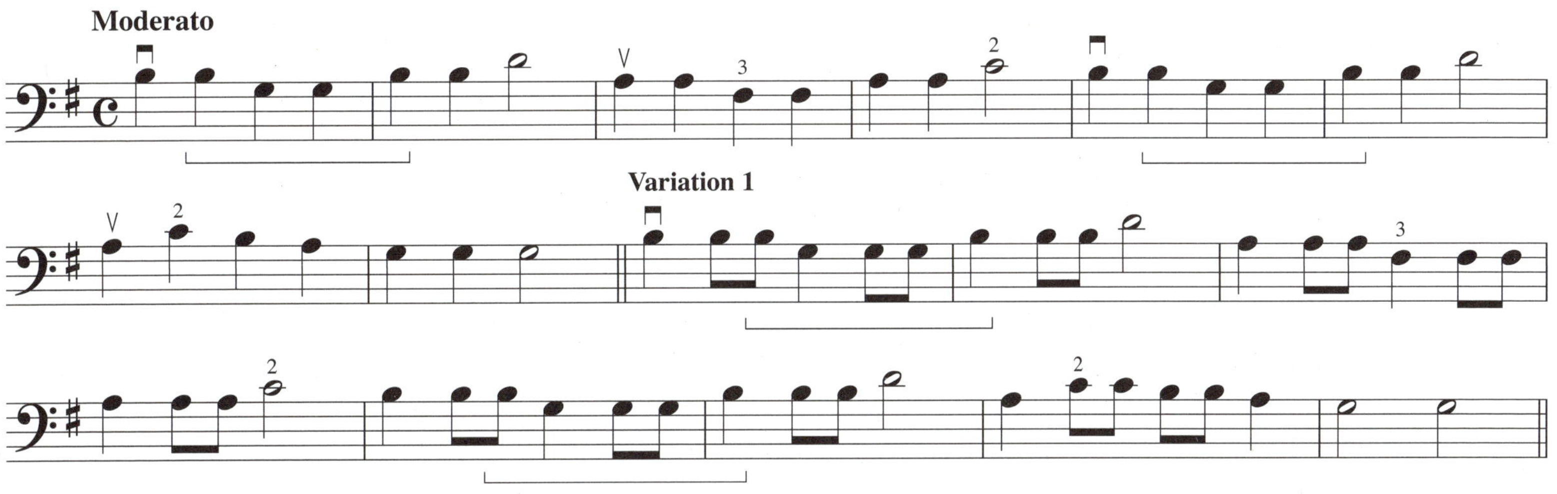

Variation 2 – *make up your own variation*

143. ESSENTIAL CREATIVITY – THE BIRTHDAY SONG

Now play the line again and create your own rhythm.

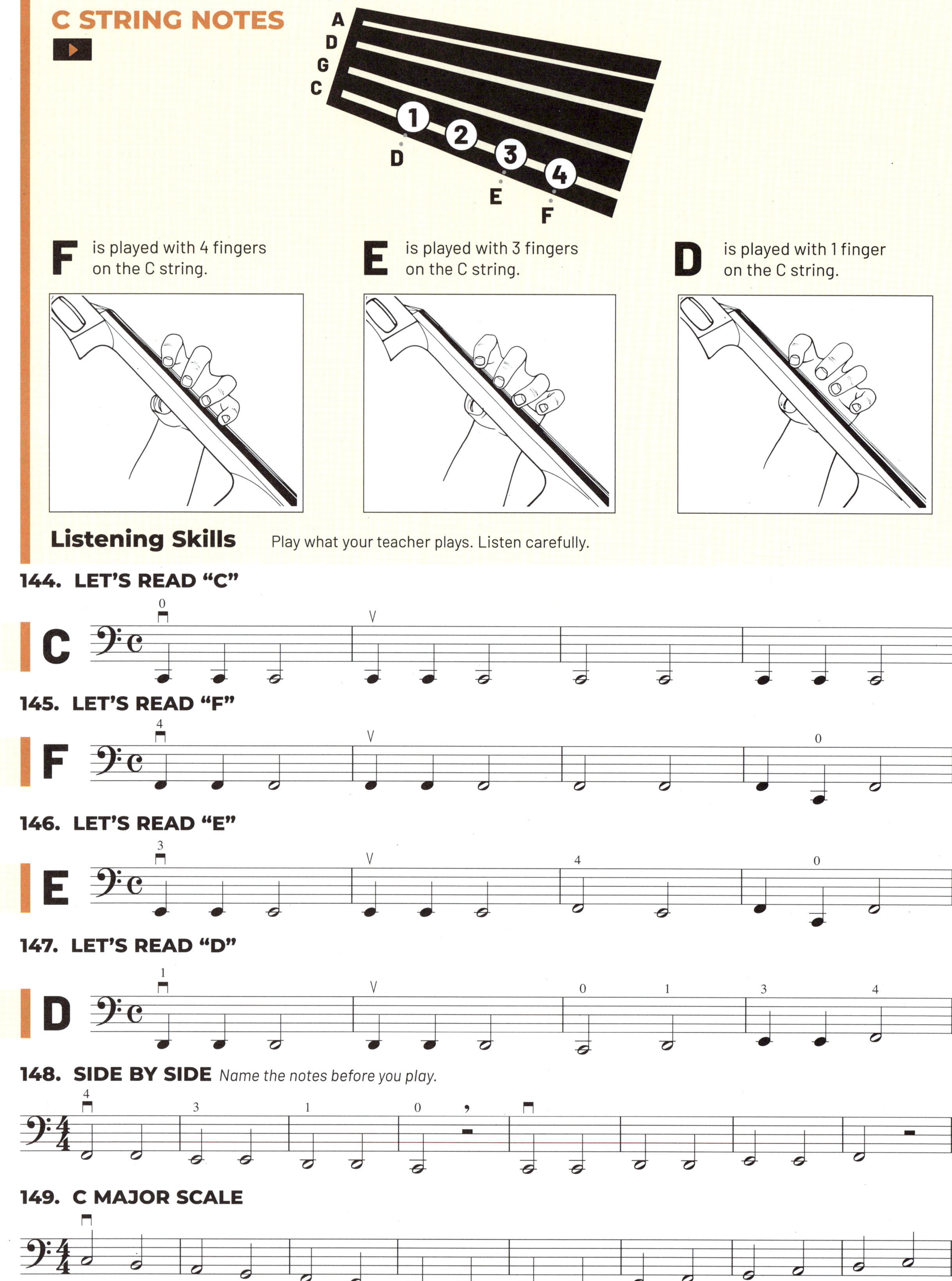
C STRING NOTES
A
D
G
C
1
2
3
4
D
E
F
F is played with 4 fingers on the C string.
E is played with 3 fingers on the C string.
D is played with 1 finger on the C string.
Listening Skills
Play what your teacher plays. Listen carefully.
144. LET'S READ "C"
C
145. LET'S READ "F"
F
146. LET'S READ "E"
E
147. LET'S READ "D"
D
148. SIDE BY SIDE
Name the notes before you play.
149. C MAJOR SCALE

Whole Note
= 4 Beats
1 & 2 & 3 & 4 &
Whole Rest
= A Whole Measure of Silent Beats
1 & 2 & 3 & 4 &
Whole Rest
hangs from a staff line.
Half Rest
sits on a staff line.
THEORY
150. RHYTHM RAP
Shadow bow and count before playing.
Count: 1 & 2 & 3 & 4 & 1 & 2 & 3 & 4 & 1 & 2 & 3 & 4 & 1 & 2 & 3 & 4 & 1 & 2 & 3 & 4 & 1 & 2 & 3 & 4 &
151. SLOW BOWS
Slow Bow
Slow Bow
Slow Bow
152. LONG, LONG AGO
T. H. Baily
Moderato
Arpeggio
An **arpeggio** is a chord whose pitches are played one at a time.
Your first arpeggio uses the 1st, 3rd, 5th, and 8th steps from the C major scale.
THEORY
153. C MAJOR SCALE AND ARPEGGIO
Arpeggio
154. LISTEN TO OUR SECTIONS
Violin
Viola
Cello
Bass
Vln.
Vla.
Vcl.
Bs.
All
155. MONDAY'S MELODY
Traditional Folk Song
Moderato
Fine
D.C. al Fine

Special Cello Exercise

Write the note names below. Then, write stories using as many note names as possible. Share your work with orchestra friends.

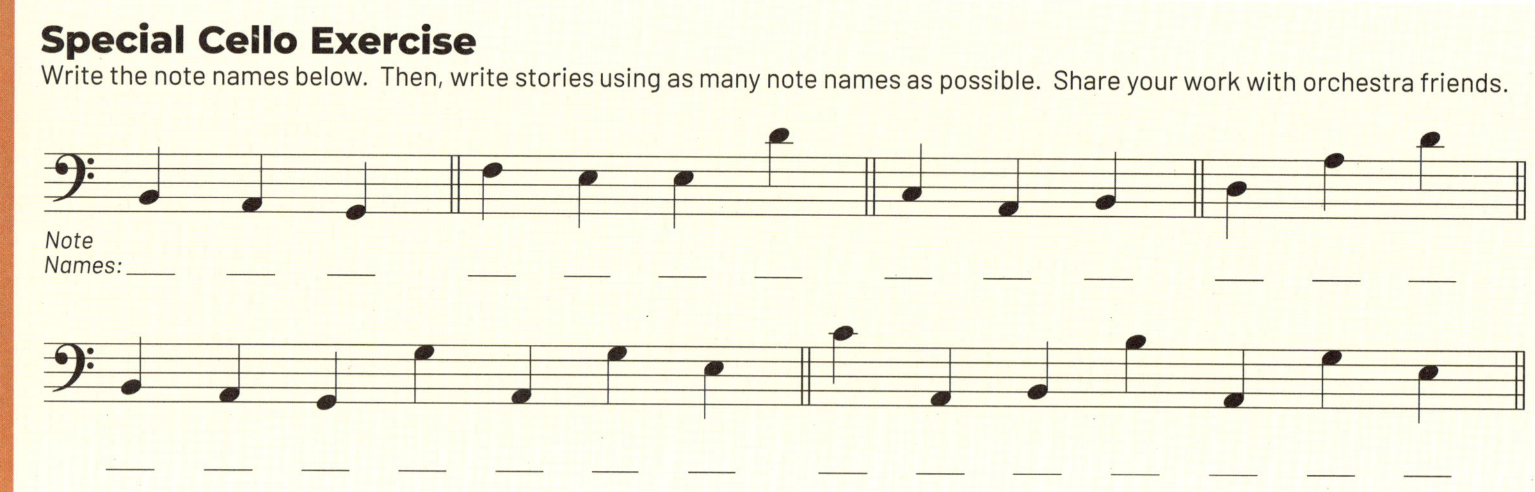

Team Work

Great musicians give encouragement to their fellow performers. Violin and bass players will now learn new challenging notes. The success of your orchestra depends on everyone's talent and patience. Play your best as these sections advance their musical technique.

Listening Skills

Play what your teacher plays. Listen carefully.

156. LET'S READ "E" – Review

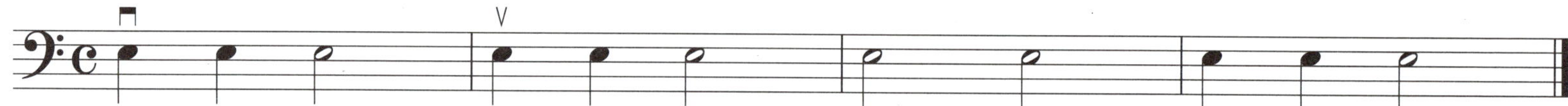

157. LET'S READ "A" – Review

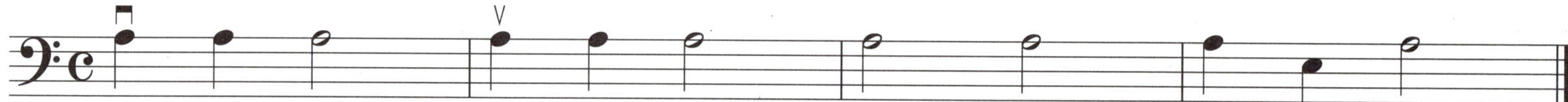

158. LET'S READ "G" – Review

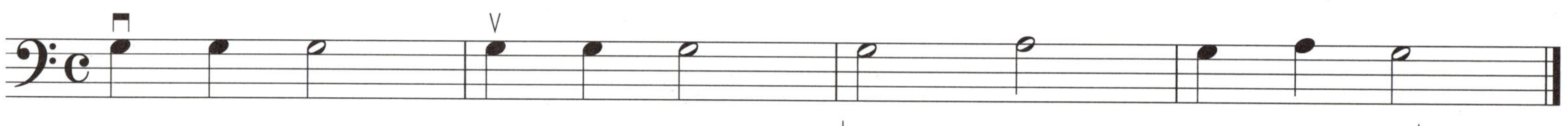

159. LET'S READ "F♯" (F-sharp)

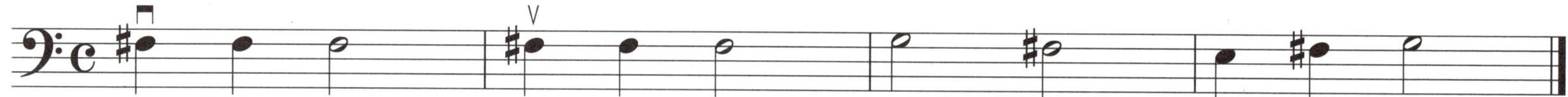

160. MOVING ALONG *Name the notes before you play.*

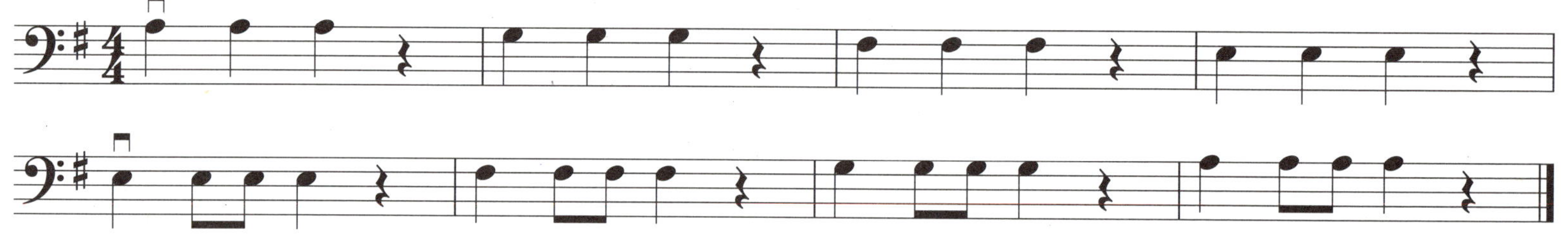

161. G MAJOR SCALE

162. SHEPHERD'S HEY

English Folk Song

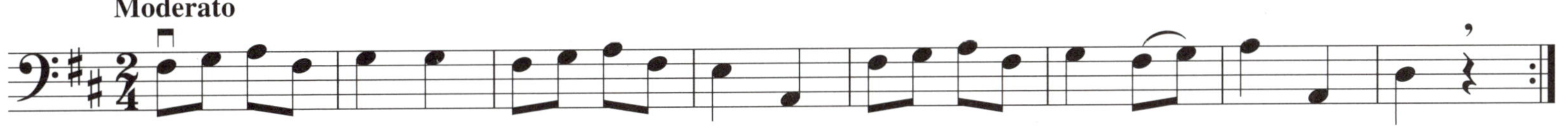

163. BIG ROCK CANDY MOUNTAIN

American Folk Song

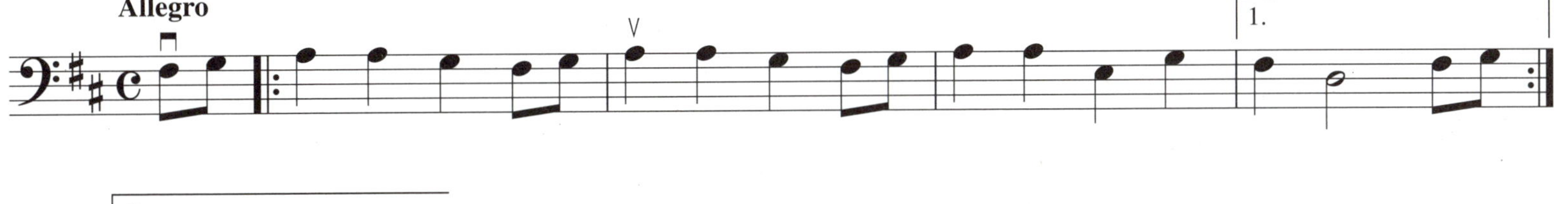

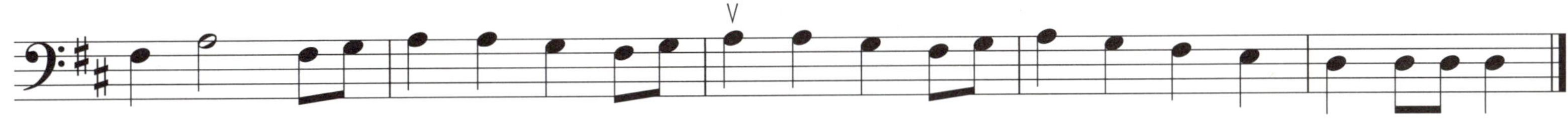

Listening Skills Play what your teacher plays. Listen carefully.

164. LET'S READ "B" – Review

165. ICE SKATING

166. ESSENTIAL ELEMENTS QUIZ – ACADEMIC FESTIVAL OVERTURE THEME

Johannes Brahms

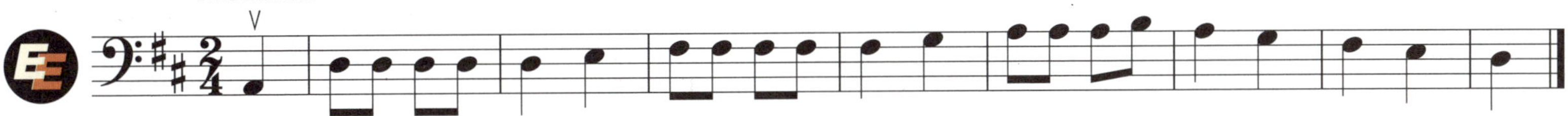

Additional bonus songs are available online. See the inside front cover for details.

Staccato ♩ or ♩ **Staccato** notes are marked with a dot above or below the note. A staccato note is played with a stopped bow stroke. Listen for a space between staccato notes. 

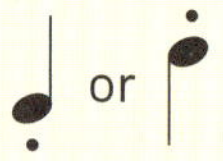

167. PLAY STACCATO

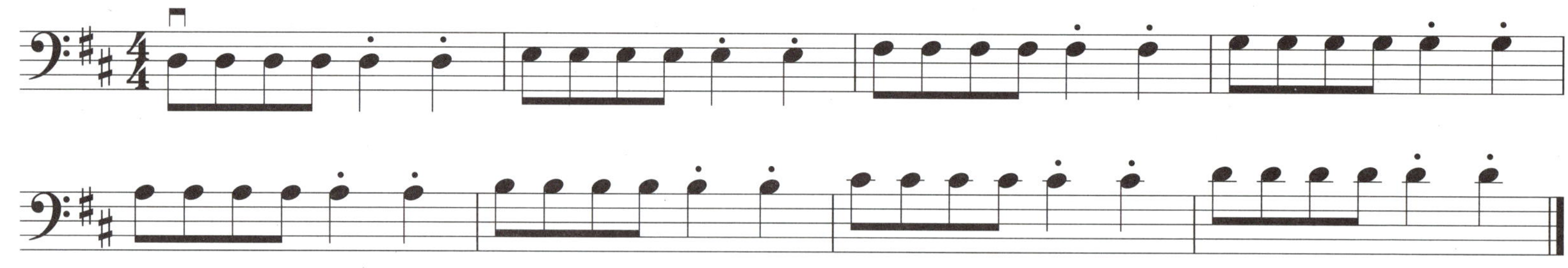

168. ARKANSAS TRAVELER

Southern American Folk Song

SKILL BUILDERS – G Major

169.

170.

171.

172.

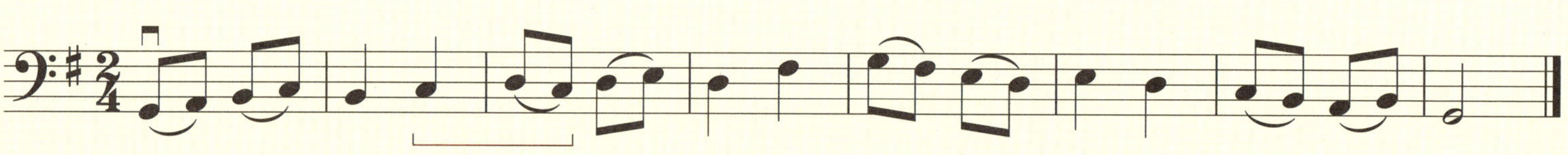

173.

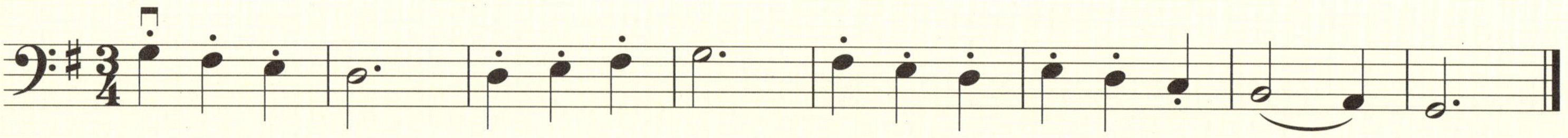

Hooked Bowing

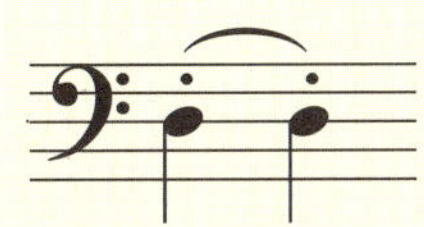

Hooked bowing is two or more notes played in the same direction with a stop between each note. 

174. HOOKED ON D MAJOR

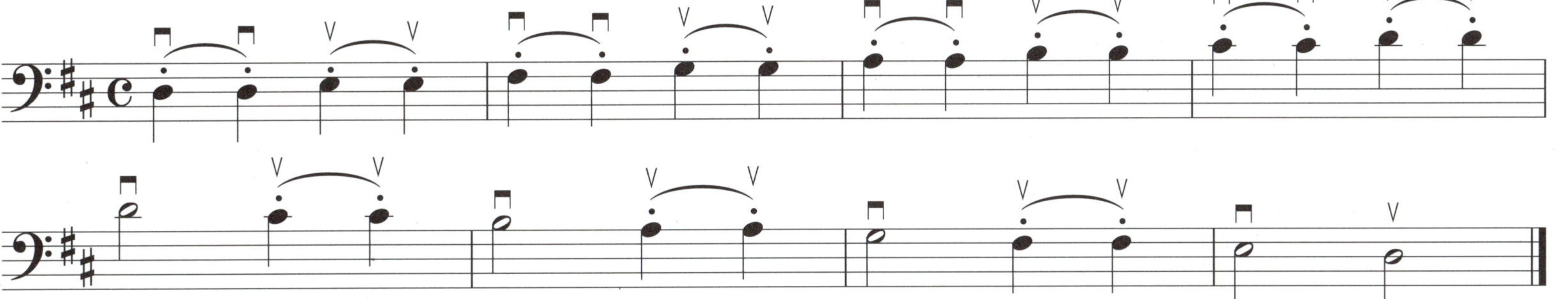

175. WALTZING BOWS

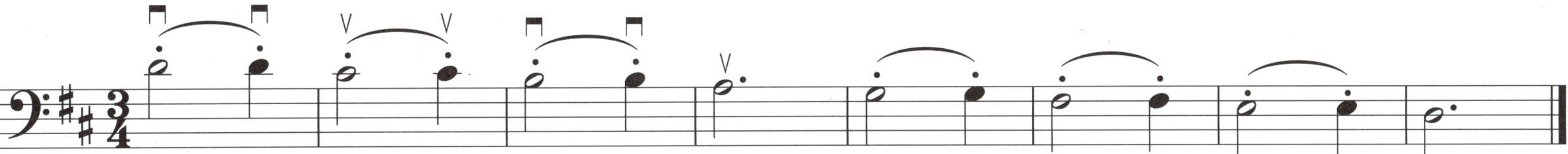

176. POP GOES THE WEASEL

American Folk Song

SKILL BUILDERS – C Major

Dynamics

Dynamics tell us what volume to play or sing.

f (*forte*) Play loudly. Add more weight to the bow.

p (*piano*) Play softly. Remove weight from the bow.

181. FORTE AND PIANO

f *p*

182. SURPRISE SYMPHONY THEME

Franz Josef Haydn

Andante

p 5 2 3 9 *f* *p* 13 *f*

SKILL BUILDERS – Scales and Arpeggios

Add your own dynamics to any of the lines below.

183. D MAJOR

184. G MAJOR

185. G MAJOR *(Upper Octave – violin)*

186. C MAJOR

187. C MAJOR

PERFORMANCE SPOTLIGHT

188. CRIPPLE CREEK – Orchestra Arrangement (**A** = Melody and **B** = Harmony)

American Folk Song
Arr. Michael Allen

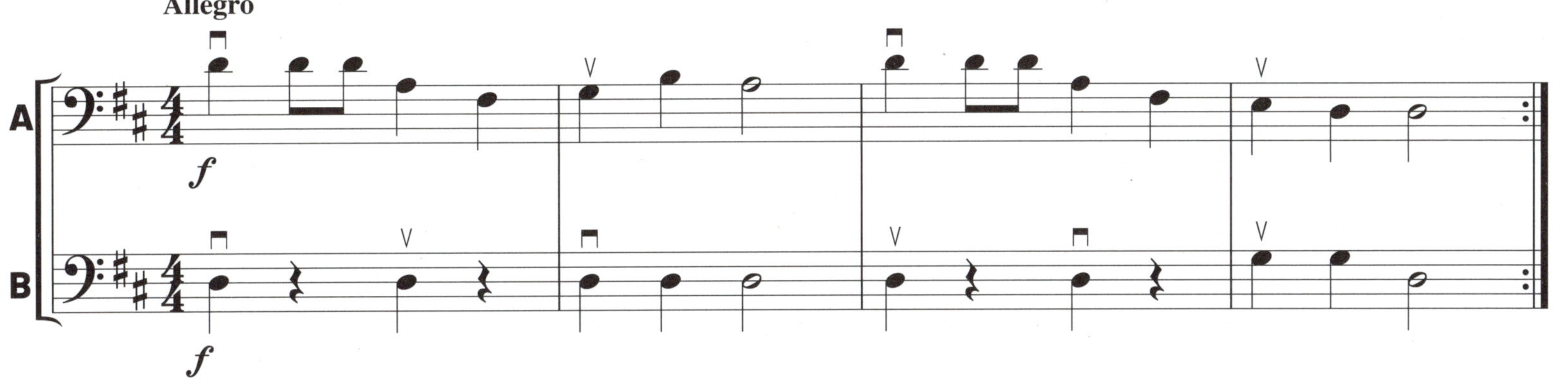

HISTORY

Africa is a large continent made up of many nations, and African folk music is as diverse as its many cultures. This folk song is from Kenya. The words describe warriors as they prepare for battle. Listen to examples of African folk music and describe the sound.

189. TEKELE LOMERIA – Orchestra Arrangement

Kenyan Warrior Song
Arr. John Higgins

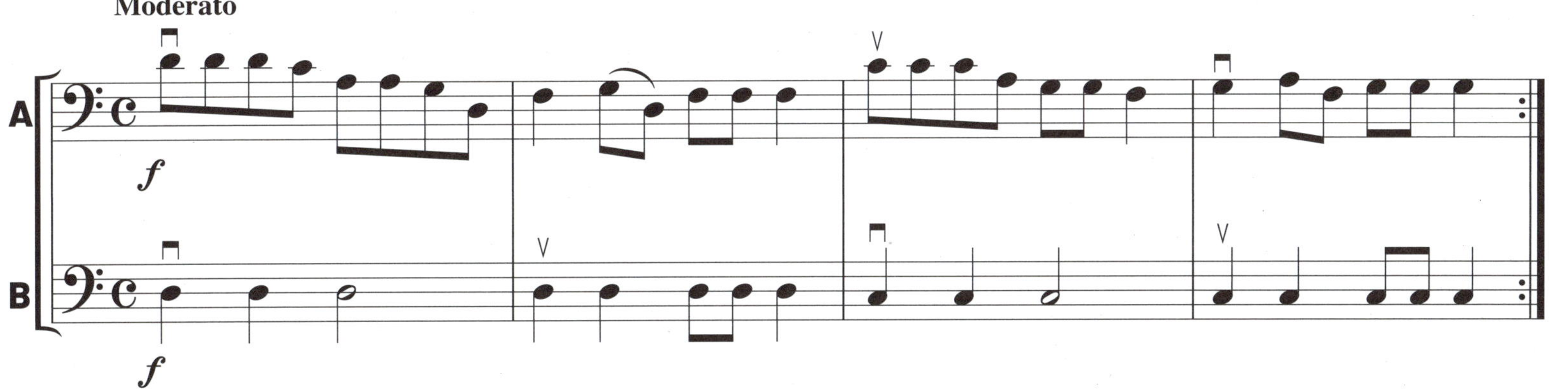

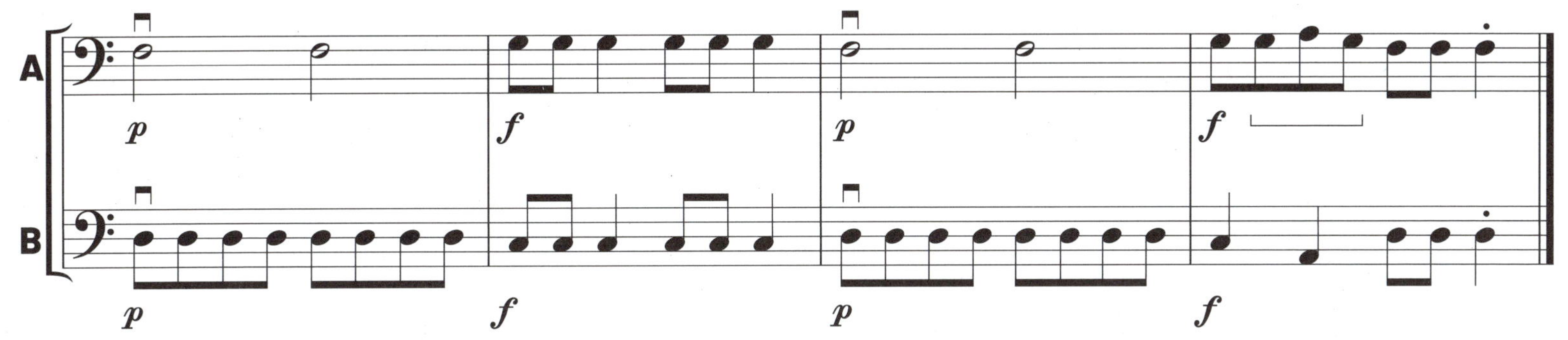

PERFORMANCE SPOTLIGHT

HISTORY

Italian composer **Gioachino Rossini** (1792–1868) wrote some of the world's favorite operas. "William Tell" was Rossini's last opera, and its popular theme is still heard on television.

190. WILLIAM TELL OVERTURE – Orchestra Arrangement

Gioachino Rossini
Arr. John Higgins

Allegro

A
B
p
f
Fine
9
D.C. al Fine

191. ROCKIN' STRINGS – Orchestra Arrangement

John Higgins

Moderato

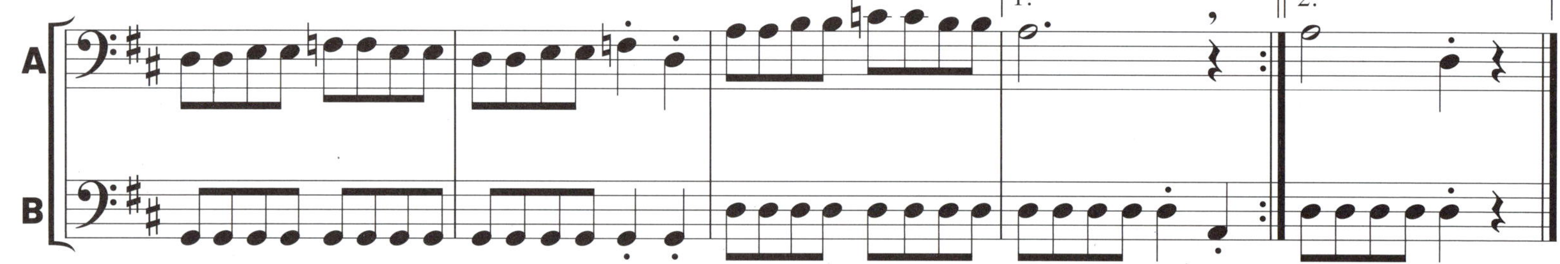

PERFORMANCE SPOTLIGHT

192. SIMPLE GIFTS – Orchestra Arrangement

Shaker Folk Song
Arr. John Higgins

Andante

A B

f *p* 10 19

PERFORMANCE SPOTLIGHT

Solo with Piano Accompaniment

A solo is a composition written for one player, often with piano accompaniment. This solo was written by **Johann Sebastian Bach** (1685–1750). You and a piano accompanist can perform for the orchestra, your school, your family and other occasions. When you have learned the piece well, try memorizing it. Performing for an audience is an excellent part of being involved in music.

193. MINUET NO. 2 – Solo

Johann Sebastian Bach
Arr. by John Higgins

Improvisation

Improvisation is the art of freely creating your own music as you play.

194. RHYTHM JAM *Using the following notes, improvise your own rhythms.*

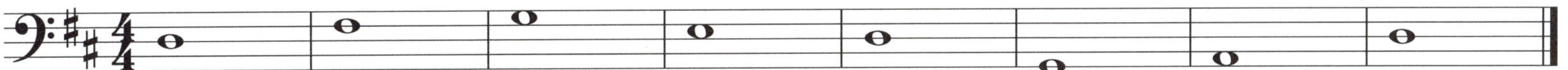

195. INSTANT MELODY *Using the following notes, improvise your own melody (Line A), to go with the accompaniment (Line B).*

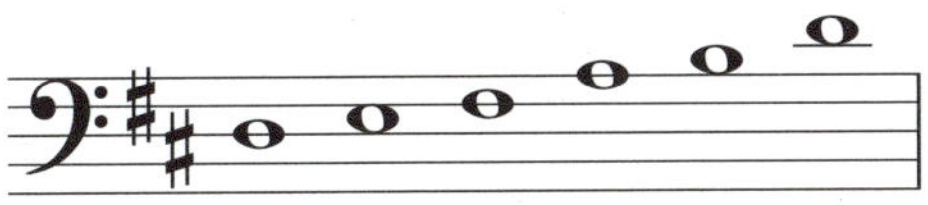

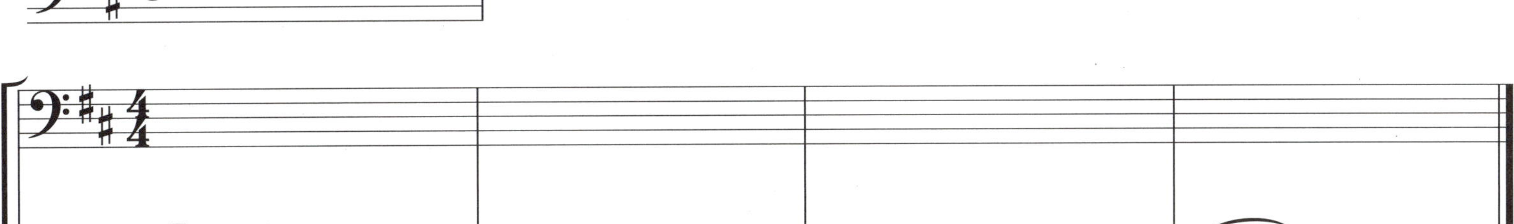

CELLO FINGERING CHART

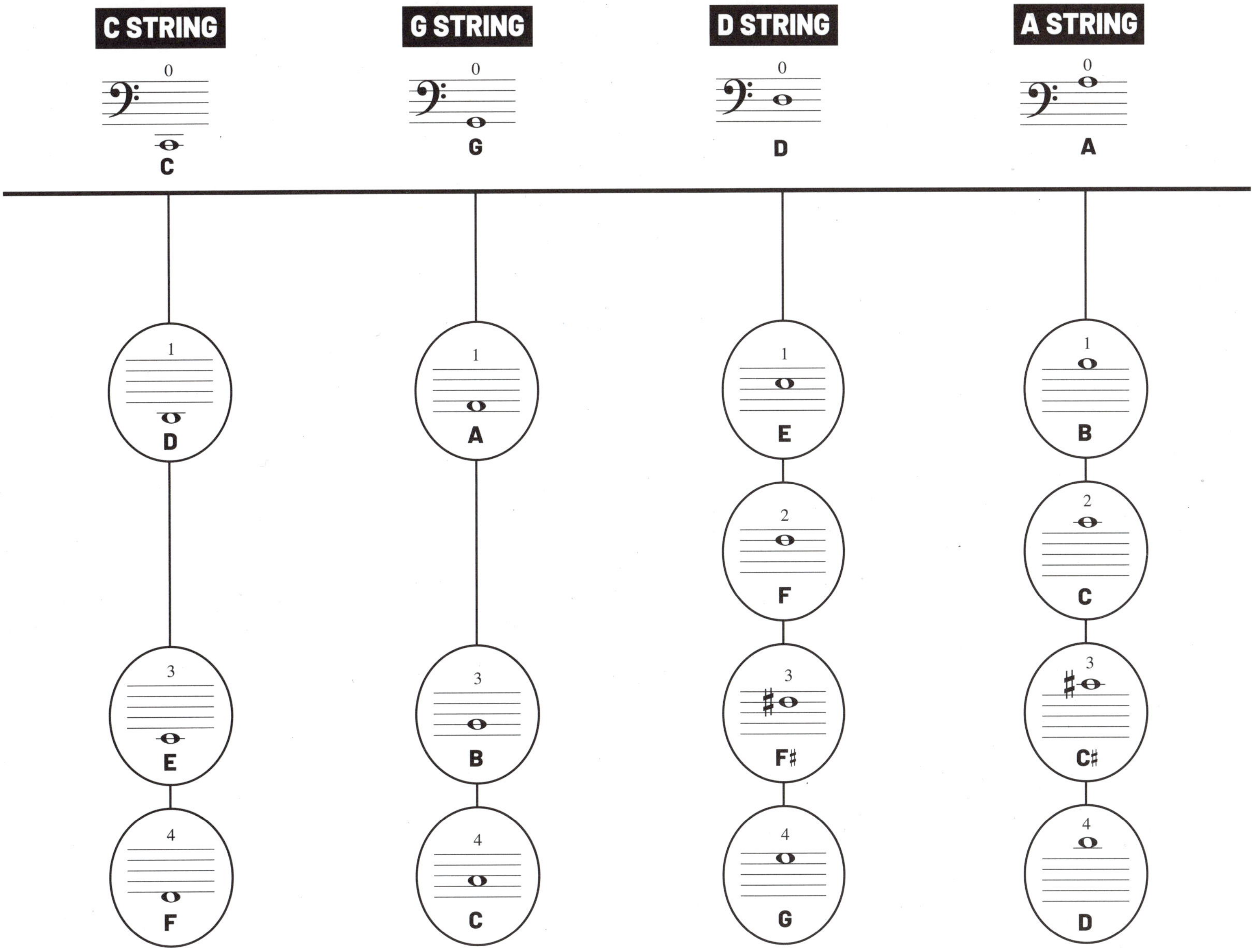

C STRING	G STRING	D STRING	A STRING
0 C	0 G	0 D	0 A
1 D	1 A	1 E	1 B
		2 F	2 C
3 E	3 B	3 F♯	3 C♯
4 F	4 C	4 G	4 D

Reference Index

Definitions (pg.)

Composers

World Music